MY PRISON LIFE

A Blogger's Insights
from the Inside

Martin L. Lockett

Copyright © 2019 by Martin L. Lockett.

All rights reserved. No part of this publication may be reproduced, distributed, or transmitted in any form or by any means, including photocopying, recording, or other electronic or mechanical methods, without the prior written permission of the author, except in the case of brief quotations embodied in critical reviews and certain other noncommercial uses permitted by copyright law.

Printed in the United States of America.

Library of Congress Control Number: 2018904724

ISBN	Paperback	978-1-64361-768-8
	eBook	978-1-64361-769-5

Westwood Books Publishing LLC
10389 Almayo Ave, Suite 103
Los Angeles, CA 90064

www.westwoodbookspublishing.com

*To all those who are personally impacted
by incarceration*

"We must never forget that we may also find meaning in life even when confronted with a hopeless situation, when facing a fate that cannot be changed. For what then matters is to bear witness to the uniquely human potential at its best, which is to transform a personal tragedy into a triumph, to turn one's predicament into a human achievement. When we are no longer able to change a situation - we are challenged to change ourselves."

— Viktor Frankl

CONTENTS

Foreword ix
Introduction xi

PART I
Adapting to Prison

Prisonsick 3
If You Love Me 5
Glass Half Full 8
Country Club or State Prison? 10
Playing Mind Games 12
It Could Always be Worse 14
Hypocrisy of Prison Politics 16
Six-Month Shakeup 18
Wishing My Life Away 20
Tuning Out 22
Splashed with Cold Water 24
Longing for Independence 26
FDA Disapproved 28
Time to Spread 31
Where are they Now? 33
A Rainbow Awaits 35
A Moment of Humanity 37
The Streets Don't Love You 39

Defying the Odds 41
Friends in Low Places 43
Falling into Place 46
Inmate Healthcare 48

PART II
Maximizing Your Potential Behind Bars

My Rock Bottom 53
No More Excuses! 55
How Much is Too Much? 57
I Will Not Become "Institutionalized" 59
Feed What Feeds You 61
Navigate the Jungle 63
Still Thankful 65
Divine Intervention 67
A Reason to be Selfish 69
Retribution or Rehabilitation? 72
Incarcerated Mentality 74
Obstacles = Opportunities 76
Camouflaged Blessings 78
A Purpose for Everything 80
Jailhouse Religion 82
God, Grant Me the Serenity 84
If I Can Do It 86
Down Payment 89
Making Payments 91
My Therapy 93
Let's be Honest 95
Inmates Giving Back 97
A Story that Needed to be Told 99
Validation 101
You Never Know Who's Watching 103

3795 Days...105
A Breath of Fresh Air 107
The Community Cares....................................109
Choices, Chances, Changes 112
Behind the Mask..115
It Starts with an Education 117
Compassionate Criminals................................120
Simply Human 123

PART III
Maintaining Romance Beyond the Bars

She's 'Doing Time' Too....................................127
Communication is the Key..............................129
Bend but Don't Break......................................131
Not Looking Back..132
Why Women Love Bad Boys 134
Are You Asking or Demanding?......................136
Follow Your Heart 138
It's The Little Things that Matter 140
She Makes Me Better 142
Intimacy: The Other Kind...............................144
Best of Teammates 146
Why She Stays 148
Why Did I Get Married?.................................150
If Roles Were Reversed 152
I Don't Wanna Know 154
It's All About Timing 156
Dear John..158
What Difference Does it Make?......................161
He Doesn't Deserve You..................................163
Worth Waiting For 165
It's Nothing Personal.......................................167

He's Just Using You . . . or is He? 169
Still Room to Grow................................171
They'll Never Understand............................173
Advantages of a Prison Relationship 175
She's Better than I Deserve 177
Love Is 179

PART IV
The Ripple Effect

A Pebble in the Pond................................183
The Power of a Letter 185
Let Them Love You 187
The Agony of a Visit.................................189
Disconnected 191
Mom, It's Not Your Fault 193
A Meal I Won't Forget 195
The Time is Never Enough............................197
An Oasis in a Barbed-Wire Desert 199
All About the Kids 201
Where has the Time Gone?............................203
A Fish out of Water..................................205
Branded 207
Something I'll Never Adapt To.........................210
Adopt an Inmate....................................212
Letter to My Younger Self.............................215

FOREWORD

> *"It may be that when we no longer know what to do, we have come to our real work and when we no longer know which way to go, we have begun our real journey. The mind that is not baffled is not employed. The impeded stream is the one that sings."*
>
> *- Wendell Berry*

In the summer of 2013, a bomb went off in my family, when my brother was arrested for a crime he didn't commit. Nearly six years later in May of 2019, he was released on parole. Everything in my life is measured by what came before the explosion, and what came after.

What came after the initial shockwave and its aftermath of anguish was the sluggish process of healing. The road to acceptance was littered with wreckage – and we arrived shell-shocked, dusty and disheveled – changed, but intact. With my brother's direction (while still incarcerated) and the help of a small army of angels, we formed a non-profit to help others touched by the criminal justice system.

Fast forward to the Fall of 2015. Adopt an Inmate was in its infancy, and we had just begun to correspond with inmates at Oregon State Correctional Institution. Our staff researcher (a.k.a., my mother) brought to my attention an inmate survey submitted by one Martin Lockett - a published author and GED tutor, with a Bachelor's degree in Sociology and a few credits away from a Master's degree in Psychology.

I'm always looking for talented writers to contribute content for the website - so I promptly ordered his book and wrote to him. Within weeks we published the first of many blog posts and book reviews written by Martin.

His life experience, coupled with a formal education, lends itself to informed writing that helps inmates adapt to prison and better themselves. I continue to rely on his support of, and contributions to our organization - and count him among my dearest of friends. More than that - his mission to live his life tirelessly, with total commitment and in honor of his victims, earned my lifelong respect.

What Martin had learned, before my family and I were forced to learn it, is that our afflictions are inseparable from our gifts. A meaningful life is not marked by the absence of loss or tragedy - but rather our response to tragedy of living gracefully in its wake. In that grit of existence, Martin's greatest freedom came to him.

If you are holding this book, you may be one of the millions of Americans caught in the grip of the justice system. Martin's life is evidence that you are not limited by your circumstance, that you also can emerge from the debris of catastrophe and grief, with value to offer the world.

Melissa Schmitt
She-EO, Adopt an Inmate
Veneta, Oregon

INTRODUCTION

Fourteen years ago, at the age of twenty-four, I sat in a county jail facing twenty years in prison. I had no idea how I was going to get through what inevitably lay before me. My emotions were mired in grief, disbelief, and sheer agony. I was also forced to contemplate my own future of being away from my parents and siblings for what would surely be a lot more than a decade. I was a mess. I was in shambles. As far as I was concerned, my life had ended abruptly; it was over for me — or so I thought.

Almost a year later, I would discover my fate. It would be a mandatory seventeen-and-a-half-year sentence — day for day. After passing through all five phases of grief from such a traumatic loss, I knew I had to pull myself together and decide what I was going to do for the next seventeen years. I knew I'd have to do a thorough search of myself to make the next almost two decades of my life count. If nothing else, I was determined to leave prison a much better, more mature man at the age of forty-two than the one who entered it at twenty-four.

Through this process of intense introspection, I developed a burning desire to counsel young men who come from a background like mine — impoverished and crime-stricken — and particularly those who struggle with substance addiction. So, I set out to get a college education and was able to do so by taking one class per term as the prison allowed. The program offered classes for only $25 each because funding from private donors paid the rest of the cost for the classes through a local community college.

In that time, I was also blessed and fortunate enough to meet an amazing woman who took a deep interest in my passions and wanted to help me achieve my goal of attaining a degree. Through her diligent research efforts, I was able to enroll in several degree programs via correspondence and went on to earn a Certificate of Human Services from Louisiana State University, AA from Indiana University, and a BS in Sociology from Colorado State University-Pueblo. Furthermore, I recently earned my Master of Science in Psychology from California Coast University. Without question, I would not be where I am today academically (over twelve years later) without her tremendous support, encouragement, and unwavering belief in me and my dreams.

As a GED tutor in the education departments at two prisons for over ten years now, I have also had the pleasure of being able to assist other men with their education. By working with men of all ages, races, and backgrounds, I have been able to capitalize on many opportunities to both teach and be taught. We all have a stake in the educational pool of life.

My fiancée has inspired me to do many things, but I nearly thought her faith in my abilities had reached a point of fantastical optimism when several years ago she suggested I write a book — my life story no less! After I immediately dismissed her over-the-top suggestion as unrealistic, she didn't bring it up again — at least not for a while. When she did bring it up again a few months later, however, voicing her enthusiastic belief in me and the need for me to share my story of hope and optimism through extreme adversity, I felt differently. I listened more intently and agreed with her rationale that it might be worthwhile to get my story out to those who could benefit by hearing what I had endured and overcome, while staying positive through it all. I undertook this project, and *Palpable Irony: Losing my freedom to find my purpose* was published three years later.

Throughout the process of writing my life story, I learned a great deal about myself as I reflected on my adolescent behavior and the faulty beliefs I relied on to justify it. It was through that process that I began to view writing somewhat differently; it became the conduit through which I could capture my innermost thoughts and reflections

MY PRISON LIFE

as I underwent this ongoing metamorphosis of self-discovery and expanding intelligence. I needed more. I needed a voice that would reach beyond my immediate surroundings and even beyond that of the book that would be read by many. Little did I know, I would soon be afforded that opportunity.

About three months after *Palpable Irony* was published, I received a letter from a woman who had read it and wanted to tell me her thoughts. She appreciated how "raw and honest" the book was and felt it could be a "catalyst to change lives." Humbled by her thoughtful response, I eagerly replied to her letter; that became the beginning of a regular correspondence and friendship.

A couple letters later, she asked me what I would like to do when I got out, so I told her it was my passion to counsel adolescents but to also do some public speaking — anything to help change lives. She then asked me if I would be interested in blogging while I was still incarcerated, and she offered to post the entries for me. Initially, I was reluctant to do so because I had never written a blog post, nor had I any idea of what a blog was comprised of. But I remained open to the idea because I still had an insatiable desire to write for an audience.

About a month later a correctional officer slid a large manila envelope underneath my door at mail delivery time. Noticing it was from my new pen pal, I became excited because I knew there would be interesting contents inside — and there were. She had sent several printouts of information on how to write a blog, the purpose of a blog, and other pertinent information that would get me started in this endeavor. I felt I had what it took to do this after all. Later that night I wrote my first blog post.

She would post my blogs on her Inmates Matter Too (IMT) website, a platform for families and friends of those incarcerated to receive support and advice on how to best navigate their tough circumstance. I was honored to write blogs three days a week for this audience as I felt I had gained considerable insight over the years that would both help them better understand prison dynamics and politics, as well as offer insight they could pass along to their incarcerated loved ones that would help them through their prison journey. I wrote about things that I witnessed on a daily basis that I objected to or found inspiring. I blogged about relationships and how things are perceived from both the woman's perspective as well as her confined mate's vantage point. I wrote about the difficulties of visiting family and friends, adjusting to prison in general, and committing to changing one's stubborn thinking patterns and using prison to better oneself. Truthfully, I don't think there's much that I *didn't* write about! The topics are vast and the content is rich. The responses from followers of the blog were very encouraging and appreciated; they both humbled and motivated me to continue writing.

Many readers informed me that they were printing the blog posts from the website to mail to their imprisoned loved ones. This prompted the idea to comprise a book from those first 100 blog posts so the friends and family of those incarcerated would easily be able to send them directly to their incarcerated loved ones.

It is my hope that all of you who have purchased this book for either yourself or someone incarcerated will gain insight and encouragement to help you through your challenging time. Every word was written for you with the intention of providing perspective and perhaps another way of approaching the arduous journey ahead, one that will surely test your patience and perseverance. May the words written throughout this book meet you where you are to fill you with hope, invigoration, insight, and motivation to overcome the physical barriers and mental challenges that confront you and your loved ones during their incarceration.

PART I

Adapting to Prison

PRISONSICK

I never knew it was possible to be "homesick" from prison — what a paradox! (Or so I thought). But that's exactly what happened to me when I transferred to a new prison after serving nearly ten years in the same facility.

Within hours of my arrival, I felt depressed and in disarray. Tantamount to being free, we prisoners often become comfortable, complacent, and even begin to take for granted, dare I say, the few luxuries our confines have afforded us. For example, I came from living in an incentive housing unit (reserved for inmates who exhibit good behavior for a minimum of 18 consecutive months) where I enjoyed privileges such as access to a microwave and soda machine, all-day yard and phone availability, daily showers, and haircuts as often as I liked, among other things. Well, I was in for a rude awakening when I arrived here at my new prison and discovered I could only shower every other day, make one ten-minute phone call per evening, get my hair cut once a month, could not go to yard in the mornings, could not use napkins or paper towels during meals, had no access to dayroom areas, and had sacrificed other minor luxuries I had grown accustomed to over the years. I couldn't believe I had volunteered to relocate and change my comfortable living for *this!*

As I experienced this acute anxiety and self-pity, all I wanted was to hear a familiar voice from my family and friends or see their faces. I was unable to make a call my first night due to there being only five phones available to accommodate over two hundred inmates! But when I was finally able to make a call the next day, a huge sense of relief and comfort swept over me. After all, I *did* volunteer to come here to be much closer to my family so they could visit me more frequently and easily.

It has now been over a month, and I have settled in a lot more and feel like this won't be so hard after all. It took that much-needed familiarity from family and friends to settle me, assure me it would be okay, and encourage me to embrace my new situation. Therefore, if I can offer any advice to people who have a friend or family member who has either just become incarcerated or has recently moved to another prison, it is simply to be there for them. A mere phone call or encouraging letter can make all the difference in the world. Assure them that it will be okay. I understand that ongoing regular support can be burdensome, so I'm not necessarily underscoring that here. All I'm saying is that it will help them immensely, both psychologically and emotionally, if you show them you care during their tumultuous transition.

IF YOU LOVE ME

I cannot tell you how many times I've been on the phone while regrettably being forced to listen to another inmate on the phone next to me scold his girlfriend or mother for not doing something he had asked them to do. "Why haven't you sent the money? . . . you said you'd send it a week ago! You're worthless!" Or the classic, "If you love me . . . " only to manipulate the poor soul on the other end of the phone into feeling guilty for not doing something in a "timely" fashion.

Sadly, this mentality is prevalent in prison. It appears that when people come to prison they automatically expect the world to stop, wait for them, and make itself available on a moment's notice for whatever they need. When they call, they expect people they claim to love to stop what they're doing to do something they've asked – right then and there. There's no consideration or allowance for what their loved one is doing because it's all about them.

I have been in prison for over twelve years, and I have managed to keep myself extremely busy and productive throughout this time. I've earned certificates and degrees from major universities via correspondence, published a book, blogged regularly, and much more. I, unequivocally, could not have done any of this without the help from those on the outside who love and support me in what I am doing to better my life. But I do not operate from the fallacious, arrogant notion that they *owe* me their time and assistance. And the reason why this is never my assumption is because I accept the reality that they didn't put me here — *I did!* It was me and me alone who decided to break the law and come to prison! How does that translate to others now owing it to me to alter their lives in any way to come to my aid? Sure, I ask for their help and certainly appreciate it when they give it, but I don't take it for granted; in no way do I take advantage of their love and commitment to me by beginning a request with the cunning words, "If you love me . . . " This is nothing but a manipulative tactic to get people to do what you want. In its extreme form, it is pathological and sociopathic.

Quite frankly, it infuriates me to hear inmates say these things to their families and loved ones, or to generous people like those who operate organizations such as Adopt an Inmate and IMT. It is the selflessness and compassion that these people freely offer out of the goodness of their hearts to those of us who messed up and put ourselves in prison that bring a rare quality to our lives while here. So, to hear people who are extremely ungrateful scold someone because something wasn't done "soon enough" or the way "it should have been done" is nothing short of despicable. I always feel the instinctive urge to shout in these people's ear, *"They didn't put you in prison – you did!"* But this would be futile, and I'll explain why.

Those who take advantage of others do so from a position of self-centeredness. This is a classic symptom of immaturity that has its roots in insecurity. Furthermore, I venture to say that most of us who are in prison have operated from this standpoint for most of our lives, thus we engaged in behavior that was destructive to ourselves and others while considering no one's feelings but our own. Because of this insatiable drive to meet our needs – often at the expense of others – being in prison has only magnified it. Why? Glad you asked.

The reason why prison brings out the worst in those who still suffer from this undeveloped mindset is because now we are entirely dependent on others! We cannot do for ourselves even the most basic things, so our legitimate dependency is now at the forefront of our existence. This causes the person who is already inclined to expect others to meet their every need to be even more aggressive in this pursuit. Their strategic tactics become more pronounced and deceitfully crafted to get their way. Trying to use the logic of argument that they put themselves here and therefore no one is responsible to take care of them falls on deaf ears because this would require a level of accountability and responsibility that they do not possess. And that's why you get, "If you love me . . ."

I am grateful for all those who have sacrificed a tremendous amount of their time and effort to make my life easier and more productive over the last twelve years. I could not have done half the things that I have without their help. But make no mistake, they owe me nothing – I put *myself* here!

GLASS HALF FULL

When faced with life's most adverse situations, there are essentially two dichotomous, opposing perspectives that people view them from: a glass half empty or half full.

These are obviously metaphors to describe how we typically view and respond to challenging predicaments in life. People *choose* to approach adversity from a negative standpoint or a positive one. This, likewise, holds true for all of us who are incarcerated.

Many people would naturally only view prison from a glass-half-empty point of view. After all, no one volunteers to be here or enjoys being confined against their will. And how could this extreme, agonizing form of punishment possibly be of value, substance, or benefit to the person who is incarcerated? I would imagine we all initially viewed our incarceration from this vantage point. I certainly could not fathom finding a silver lining in this ordeal while I was awaiting trial. It wasn't until I analyzed my predicament through a different lens that I was able to find profound meaning and purpose in what lied ahead of me for the next seventeen years.

Once I had accepted the fact I was going to be here for nearly twenty years — whether I chose to deal with it constructively or not — I allowed myself to begin to focus on the positive opportunities that would present themselves, rather than choosing to dwell on the obvious negative aspect of my situation. I began to understand that this was a distinct opportunity to delve deeply into the many deep-seated underlying issues that led to my negative self-image growing up, which in turn led to my substance abuse and eventual criminality. I discovered an inner passion that I never knew existed to counsel young men who came from the same disadvantaged background as I did. I was grateful for the fact I could overcome my alcohol addiction (albeit involuntarily) through my incarceration because I knew this was the *only* way I could salvage my life and cultivate the necessary education and skills that would enable me to help others struggling with addiction. Prison saved my life and has given me a second chance to live the life God intended for me to live all along. Throughout this tragedy, I've been afforded the opportunity to earn college degrees, publish a book, and mentor many young men along the way.

I often wonder what I would be doing and what my quality of life would be had this never happened. I shudder to think what I'd be doing. When I consider what I've done during my incarceration, I'm overcome with gratitude and appreciation for what this situation has allowed me to do and become. What would have happened had I sat here feeling sorry for myself for the past eleven years? This is exactly what I mean when I say it makes an enormous difference in how we choose to approach our challenges (no matter how severe), whether we look at them from a glass-half-empty or glass-half-full perspective. Either way, I'm going to be here; it's strictly up to me how I'm going to utilize my time.

Someone once told me something, and it resonated with me so much I turned it into a motto that I applied to my life. What he told me was, "Life is ten percent what happens to you and ninety percent how you react to it." This is such a profound statement because it puts the emphasis on how *we* decide to assess and deal with life's most difficult circumstances; the emphasis is *not* on the difficulty of the circumstance itself. Two people can look at the same glass of water and reach two different conclusions. Knowing this, I've made the conscious decision to approach my incarceration and life's hardships from a glass-half-full viewpoint.

COUNTRY CLUB OR STATE PRISON?

Tomorrow afternoon a Fed Ex delivery truck will pull up to the front gate of the prison where its driver will unload boxes of merchandise and drive off to his or her next destination. The boxes will then be taken to an office where they will be unpacked, and their contents sorted and distributed according to whom ordered what. No doubt, the men who ordered the contents are overly excited to finally receive the product they paid for months ago. Oh, the contents, you ask? X-Boxes, controllers, and an assortment of video games. Oh, I'm sorry, for whom, you ask? Inmates of all kinds — murderers, rapists, and everyone in between!

Now, I can imagine the fury, indignation, and many other adjectives that could capture your profound discontentment mounting as you read this, but before you get too angry, let's talk about it. On one hand, there are those who come from the school of thought that inmates ought to eat bread and drink water three times a day for nourishment and sleep on cold slabs of concrete to serve their punishment. Then there are those who align on the opposite end of the spectrum and believe inmates ought to have access to privileges as an incentive for good behavior during incarceration, increasing the chances they will be law-abiding after release.

Regardless of your personal sentiment about how inmates should be treated while incarcerated, the fact of the matter is there is no X-Box, microwave, soda machine, vending machine, or any other luxury item we are afforded (after maintaining at least eighteen months good conduct) that can ever be enough to counter the despair of being confined to a small concrete cell every day and night. No luxury item they can offer can mitigate the loneliness we feel when we go to bed every night without being able to hug and kiss our wives/girlfriends or tuck in our children. No mp3 player, personal television, or CD player can ever give us back the many birthdays and holidays we've spent apart from our loved ones.

Prison *is* our punishment; we are not here to be punished while in prison. Furthermore, if you ask me, I'd think with ninety-five percent of all prisoners destined to return to society at some point, it does the inmate — and subsequently society at large — some good to have a reward to work toward by exhibiting good behavior. This is a simple form of behavioral therapy. If the prospect of being able to play an X-Box, have an mp3 player, or use a microwave while in prison is what starts an inmate on a path of understanding that his or her good behavior will be rewarded, then I think it's not so egregious after all. For those who believe these things actually diminish the impact of punishment that prison is designed for, and that facilities offering such luxuries end up resembling a country club more than a prison, allow me to be the first one to gladly turn in my membership for a full refund!

PLAYING MIND GAMES

"I hereby sentence you to the Oregon Department of Corrections for a duration not to exceed two hundred and ten months." This is what the judge dictated to me at the age of twenty-four. Seventeen and a half years; that's what I'd just been sentenced to. Sure, I knew in my cognitive, rational mind how long it was, but there was absolutely no way I could have fully comprehended just how long that was (in real time) to be confined and secluded from civilization until I embarked on this long journey.

Without thinking about it, after a year or two I began to subconsciously count seasons instead of years when counting down my time. I knew once I'd gone through four three-month seasons, a year had gone by. *I can do this for the rest of my sentence*, I thought. But after a few years, it just didn't seem to work like it once had; it was time to switch things up.

I could have counted holidays but decided not to do that because it was already extremely difficult to cope with holidays and being away from my family. Then, about five years into my sentence (leaving me with twelve and a half years, if you're counting), I came up with what I thought was a great psychological strategy to count down my remaining time.

When inmates would ask me how much time I had left (which I didn't really feel comfortable talking about because it was still such a long time), I'd instinctively say, "Twelve and some change." This way I could answer their question but avoid discussing exactly how much time I had left. The "change" could have meant anywhere between one and eleven months. Then I thought, *it sounds so much better to say I have a number less than what I have the day after my future release date*. For instance, on June 29th I will officially be one day under seven years remaining on my sentence, so guess what I'm going to say I have left? Exactly — "six and some change." It sounds so much better than seven years, doesn't it? It sure does to me. In fact, my loved ones have even begun counting down my time this way as well. We get excited together every June because we know it's getting closer to saying one number less than what we had been saying for the past year.

People that are incarcerated count down their time in a multitude of ways to help them feel as though the time is not as long as it actually is. I've heard guys say they count the number of haircuts (every two weeks) they have left, presidential elections, holidays, seasons, visits (monthly), Super Bowls, and a host of other significant occasions. Hey, if it works, it works! This is probably one of the only times playing mind games is not a terrible thing.

IT COULD ALWAYS BE WORSE

It could always be worse. This is a phrase we commonly use to help mitigate the psychological pain and distress we, or others, are feeling. We restructure our way of viewing the difficult circumstance by reasoning that there are always people in this world who have it much worse than we do. This tends to lessen the despair we may be feeling in that moment, while adding some much-needed comfort.

As I've previously stated, I'm serving a mandatory minimum seventeen-year sentence. It is also true that I've viewed this tragedy as my wakeup call and to make something of my life by becoming a drug and alcohol counselor to help others in their addiction. So, I've been able to maintain a positive, constructive, optimistic outlook throughout this situation. In doing so, I have also been able to fend off much of the stress and despairing feelings that typically plague inmates who are serving extremely long sentences.

Having said this, I still have my days, my moments that cause me to ask *why*? Why did I decide to drink and drive that fateful night? I do not, however, remain in this nonproductive frame of mind very long for obvious reasons, but from time to time I do wake up in the morning, stare out of my small cell window into the view of the desolate prison compound and think to myself, *I can't believe I'm still here after all these years.*

However, I snap out of this unhealthy way of thinking by quickly realizing that although a tragedy landed me here, this has been an extraordinarily positive experience thus far; that I've been able to do so many meaningful things that I likely wouldn't have done had I not

MY PRISON LIFE

come here; and there are many people around me who have it so much worse than I do. I can appreciate the fact I will be released one day to be with my family and loved ones again to live a normal, productive life in society. Sadly, there are many men here who will never have those priceless opportunities again, so why am I feeling so pitiful? It is in those moments that I become grateful for the things I have to look forward to; to understand that — albeit through a horrible tragedy — *all* things happen for a reason. Unfortunately, it took my coming to prison to make me a better man, but I'm grateful that it forced me to seriously reevaluate my life and take it in an entirely new direction.

Adopting the mentality of admitting your current circumstance could always be worse (therefore causing you to be grateful for what you *do* have, despite how challenging times may be) applies just as equally to our loved ones — those on the outside who feel immense grief due to our physical absence. Next time you're feeling sad, stressed, or angry toward the situation of your loved one being incarcerated, I strongly encourage you to change your perspective by reminding yourself that there are countless others who — believe it or not — have it much worse.

HYPOCRISY OF PRISON POLITICS

For the past eleven years, I've lived amongst society's worst criminals — rapists, robbers, murderers, molesters, and everyone in between. Yet, it still astounds me that even within this contingent of people there are many who place themselves above others in the prison social hierarchy because of the crimes they have committed relative to others' crimes.

It's no secret that many consider child molesters and rapists to be society's most degenerate, horrendous criminals. When they come to prison, they themselves are abused by other, more predatory inmates who use physical violence and extortion to intimidate and exploit them. In no way am I attempting to become an apologist for these folks (sex offenders), but I also do not believe they are inherently deserving of the unspeakable abuse they endure while in prison because of the types of crimes they have committed.

The reality is *everyone* here has at least one victim (for most of us there are more) from the crime(s) they were convicted of. This does not even consider everyone we have victimized in some way or another for countless other crimes we were not caught and convicted for. Yet, men in prison will invariably and proudly boast how they were convicted of a "good crime" versus a "bad crime" because, they say, "At least I didn't rape a woman or molest a child." Yet, murdering a father and leaving his wife and kids to fend for themselves while dealing with his death for the rest of their lives is "okay" to these men because, after all, they'll reason, "At least I didn't rape his wife or molest his kids." I'm sorry; I know I'm not the only one who sees this as a twisted rationale. If I may, I'd like to offer my opinion and psychoanalysis of why this happens.

Just as people in society do, inmates look for ways to socially elevate themselves above others when they suffer from poor self-esteem. If I can look at someone next to me and find a reason to belittle him or her, then it gives me a reason to feel better about myself because, I can reason, at least I'm not like them. The ironic and sad reality of this tactic (and defense mechanism) is it still doesn't alleviate the underlying issues of low self-esteem that plague these people. Deep down they still don't like themselves and feel inadequate in some way(s). Therefore, I believe it is this same motive that compels inmates (many of whom suffer from poor self-concept/esteem) to find fault in others to elevate their own social standing within these walls. Perhaps the larger issue here, however, is that by focusing on others' flaws, it precludes those individuals from examining and addressing their own. They do not see their own shortcomings as needing attention and correction. They even brag about how they've killed someone and take pride in taking a son from his mother, father from his children, and so forth. It simply does not bother them.

I can certainly understand if inmates don't want to befriend those who are here for sex crimes — that's their prerogative. I just staunchly disagree with the notion that anyone in prison deserves to be punished at the hands of others who have themselves broken the law and victimized many people, families, and communities in immeasurable ways.

No one is incarcerated for behaving well and following the law. We have all breeched our end of the social contract and violated societal expectations of following the law. We all have many aspects of our character that we need to work on and improve. Focusing on what others have done in order to deflect attention from our *own* shortcomings will only leave us stuck in our flawed ways.

I have never engaged in condoning or propagating prison politics because they only serve to keep one trapped in a criminal's mentality of faulty rationale. The bottom line is we *all* ought to feel a sense of shame for those we have voluntarily victimized because if we don't, we are destined to do it again.

SIX-MONTH SHAKEUP

I magine this: You move into a new neighborhood and settle into your new home. You start a new job, enroll the kids into a good school that you've already scouted, and your spouse and you develop a feasible daily routine that accommodates yourselves and the children. Things go predictably well over the course of the next six months and then without warning or provocation you incredibly receive a letter from your landlord or mortgage company telling you that an irreversible error was made when you completed the paperwork and your monthly payment has just gone up several hundred dollars! The very same day, ironically, the kids return home from school with a letter written by the principal informing you that they no longer qualify to be enrolled in that school because, technically, they no longer fall within the district as it was just changed and you're now *one* block outside the school zone. Furthermore — just when you were certain it couldn't get any worse — you go into work the next morning and your boss informs you that upper management has decided it would be in the best interest of the company to hire another person to assist you with your work, thus your hours "could" be shortened by ten to fifteen per week! Talk about a *shakeup*, right? Well this is equivalent to what I (and many others who are incarcerated) go through every six months as an Oregon State inmate.

Settling into a comfortable routine in prison is imperative for the time to pass quickly, smoothly, and productively. Believe it or not, it's much like life outside of prison in that regard, in that we shower (or don't), brush our teeth, put on our clothes, and head to work. We eat lunch on our breaks, punch the clock at closing time, and return to our housing units. We go to dinner, come back and use the phone, write letters, exercise, watch TV, read, or hang out with friends. The late evening rolls around and we depart to our cells, get ready for bed, and wake up the next day to do it all over again.

Our routines are set, and we adhere to them naturally, as most humans do, to maintain a sense of predictability and security. However, unlike those in the free world, we don't have the luxury of choosing to keep things this way for over six months at a time because the Department of Corrections has a policy that mandates their officers bid for and change posts every six months. Granted, the rules of the institution are the same regardless of which officer works the housing unit, but each one comes with their own idiosyncrasies and pet peeves that dictate how they will implement those rules while working.

Because they tell us when we can shower, use the phone, or get hot water to heat up our instant-cook food items in our cells, we are subject to a total shake up every six months when a new officer bids to work in our housing unit. This may not seem like a big deal for the inmates who rarely or never use the phone, eat hot food from the canteen, or shower daily (believe me, there are some); but for the vast majority of us this means we will be forced to adapt and alter our daily routines in order to acclimate to the new officer's demands.

Today happened to be day one of a new rotation for officers, and once again we are forced to re-adjust and conform our lives to how the new officers (a different one each shift) want to operate the unit. The times I normally make my phone calls, shower, and do other leisurely activities are subject to change, depending on when the new officers allow us to do these things.

You would think that after nearly eleven years, I'd be used to this and it wouldn't affect me, that I would be unfazed and not even comment on it; but that just isn't the case. It is upsetting and despairing to know that every six months you are at someone else's mercy in nearly every aspect of your life. You can only imagine how tumultuous it would be to go through the scenario I opened this blog with, but for many of us in prison it is our virtual reality.

WISHING MY LIFE AWAY

From the first day I was incarcerated, I couldn't wait to get out! Obviously, this is a natural response to having your freedom taken away, forcing you to live in an environment against your will for any length of time. After all, the whole purpose of incarceration is to deprive you of the things you have freely enjoyed in life; this deprivation is what makes us feel the punishment of our circumstance and, ideally, would deter us from committing crime again when we are eventually released.

The issue I have is I find myself contemplating and anticipating having my freedom back to the point that it consumes my thoughts throughout the day and I can't help but wonder if I am essentially wishing my life away. I desire to have my days, weeks, months, and years of my life whisk by as quickly as possible so I can regain my freedom and be reunited with my loved ones. Of course, there is nothing inherently wrong with longing to be free; that's certainly not my position. My point is that I believe I should be simultaneously appreciating life itself and the quality of it — even in these circumstances — because, after all, it is still my life to live and make the most of — which I most certainly do.

I imagine when I'm sixty or seventy years old I'll reflect on these years and wish I would have focused more on valuing life itself and embracing the fact I have my health and youthful vitality instead of wishing these years away — despite the circumstances. Then again (I reason with myself), which is more important: appreciating life (even in here) or being reunited with my loved ones? I honestly try my very best to do both, but I have yet to strike an ideal balance. When juxtaposing the two, there is no real comparison. So, why do I feel somewhat guilty for feeling this way?

I try to mitigate this cognitive dissonance by reasoning that God has a definitive purpose for my life that includes me spending exactly seventeen and a half years in prison to prepare me for that purpose. And I know I must not allow my attention to be diverted from this fact. When I think about it in these terms, it makes me feel more at ease with this situation and, therefore, want to develop and grow more toward that purpose in the way I believe will please God. My focus is then diverted from the dreadfulness of this circumstance and placed back on a divine understanding of it all. This indeed returns my concentration to a place where I can honestly appreciate life and the unique opportunities this rigorous journey has afforded me.

Ideally, I would like to keep my attention on what I'm ultimately here for and how I am to prepare myself for a meaningful, purposeful life beyond these walls. I am, however, human and will undoubtedly find myself in moments of tumult where my physical and mental states will override my spiritual perspective. But I also know I must maintain a purpose-filled perspective and motivation to keep from simply wishing my life away.

TUNING OUT

Often in prison (and life in general), we encounter days where we just simply want to be left alone. We want to get away from people and be in the comfort of our own solitude. Obviously, in prison we do not have the luxury of seclusion in a meaningful way, so one of the only semblances of privacy we can obtain comes by way of music.

I have always found music (primarily R&B, rap, and some alternative) to be soothing and relaxing — or excitatory, depending on my mood — but since being in prison, it has taken on an even more significant role in my life. I rely on it to mentally take me away from the chaos that permeates prison life. There is nothing like being able to attach a soundproof pair of headphones to my ears, scan the many songs on my mp3 player and play one that allows me to drown out any external noise and attend to my mood in that moment. I'll find myself lost in time when I'm walking around the track on the yard, enveloped by the melodic sound in my ears that speaks to my mood and soul the way that only music can.

I recently learned that the reason why we enjoy music so much is because when we listen and find meaning in it, it stimulates the same part of our brain that is activated when we fall in love, drink caffeine, or experience something new — otherwise known as the "pleasure pathway." Our brains register music as something we inherently find pleasurable because our emotive anatomy is stimulated by it; it releases chemicals in the brain that enable us to feel. Makes a lot of sense, if you ask me.

I shudder to think of how much more destructive men in prison would be if they had no outlet like music (and other mood de-escalators) to channel their angry/emotional states. By literally and figuratively tuning out the negative vibes, people, and influences that are endemic in prison, many prisoners have been able to remain calm, focused, and grounded — especially in moments of insane volatility.

When I'm feeling sad, I'll listen to something soothing that pierces my soul and speaks to my pain. Ironically, this is very comforting and tends to help me process these complex feelings. Conversely, when I'm out jogging or lifting weights, I'll crank up my fast-paced Hip Hop to get me going and stimulate my energy level. But the most important benefit of having music is it allows me to "get away" from my difficult, inescapable surroundings. I can be surrounded by negativity and mayhem (and I often am) yet remain emotionally unaffected by it because I have the pleasure that my music brings me. Ahhh . . . what would I ever do without it?

Without provoking a debate about what luxuries should or shouldn't be provided to those who are incarcerated, I know there are many who believe inmates should not be afforded such things as an mp3 or CD player. But when considered from the position that music has a unique capability of keeping someone focused and grounded enough to use this time constructively, is that such a bad thing? Should it then be viewed as a mere comfort item for inmates or a subtle form of therapy in one's rehabilitation efforts? Food for thought.

When I reflect on the things I've accomplished academically and personally, I can honestly say that the fact that I have been fortunate enough to be able to purchase plenty of music that is meaningful to me has been just as integral during this transformation process as reading a textbook or mentoring a young person. My music is my sanctuary, my peace of mind, and my sense of freedom while in captivity. In a place where negativity swirls about so violently and perpetually, there's nothing like having the ability to simply tune it all out.

SPLASHED WITH COLD WATER

I began working at the DMV call center located at this prison just a couple months ago. After six weeks of rigorous training, I finally began fielding calls from the public on my own and answering questions related to driver licenses and vehicle registration. For the most part, customers have been appreciative for my help and have been polite (much to my surprise, as we all know the consensus sentiment toward DMV and its employees). Most customers, however, have no idea that they're speaking with an inmate when they call, and we only divulge that information if they explicitly ask.

Today was day six of me independently answering phone calls (without a trainer by my side), and I felt confident in my ability to provide customers with accurate information without relying on the technical support that is readily available for us should we need it. Then I answered a call from a customer that took me aback and gave me a hard dose of reality — like being splashed in the face with cold water first thing in the morning!

The customer called and I offered my standard greeting: "Thank you for calling Oregon DMV; this is Martin, how may I help you?" The middle-aged sounding woman replied, "May I speak with your supervisor, please?" Knowing I would be expected to relay to my supervisor the nature of the woman's issue before transferring her, I asked, "May I ask what it pertains to, please?" Somewhat agitated now, she responded, "You're an inmate, right?" Mildly caught off guard, I managed to hold my composure and answered, "Yes, ma'am." She then reiterated, "May I have your supervisor?" Because of her vehemence, I relented on asking her what the nature of the call would be at that point and politely connected her with my supervisor. I didn't have ample time in that moment to process what had just transpired because I still had to attend to other customers. But when I got off work, I certainly did.

This was the first encounter I'd had with someone from the public in my eleven years of incarceration who had blatantly discriminated against and dismissed me merely because of where I am. Sure, I deal with correctional officers daily who treat us disrespectfully (not all of them, but a good portion in my experience), but it's less impactful coming from them because after a while, you become desensitized and come to expect it. And even though I understand in my rational mind that many people in society harbor disdain for the incarcerated, it was an entirely different thing to experience it personally.

Later that evening my cellmate and I discussed it and surprisingly ended up enjoying a huge laugh. He made light of the woman's reluctance to talk to an inmate, and it didn't take long for me to join him in taking it with a grain of salt. However, after the bellyaching laugh, I did contemplate what it really signified, which is that I can expect to face this again when I'm eventually released. Prior to today, I'd been insulated from that type of reaction for eleven years, so it was certainly a crude awakening.

After moving past the initial contempt that I held for this woman, I was able to glean the hidden message and meaning behind the challenging exchange. I came away feeling somewhat satisfied in knowing that nothing anyone says or thinks about me will ever dissuade or discourage me from pursuing my goals and dreams; that my belief in myself to make a difference in the lives of many through counseling and mentoring is unshakable and far more powerful than what someone thinks about me. In fact, it is the naysayers and haters that compel and fuel me to strive even harder!

As uncomfortable as it is to be doused with ice-cold water first thing in the morning, it does make you wide-awake and immediately alert to your surroundings. My "cold water" to the face came in the form of a customer who reminded and prepared me for what to expect when I return to society; and I'm grateful for that.

LONGING FOR INDEPENDENCE

An hour ago, I was in the yard. The sun was shining, guys were intensely engaged in numerous sporting events where they competed to win free food, and barbecue smoke permeated the mid-afternoon air. It was a festive atmosphere.

This time every year, the prison hosts many events to celebrate and commemorate the Fourth of July and to give guys an opportunity to have a full day of festivities.

As I ate the barbecue cheese burger, hot dog, and drank the ice-cold soda, however, I couldn't prevent my mind from wandering into memories from my childhood when my dad would be hovered over our homemade barbecue pit (constructed from two large metal barrels welded together), us kids playing in the yard, and other family members spontaneously showing up throughout the day to grab a plate to eat. This was a tradition that my family honored every July fourth — as well as setting off fireworks by the end of the evening.

Now, however, when I think of the literal meaning of independence on Independence Day, it means something entirely different. I long to, once again, share this holiday, barbecue, and playful festivities with my family. Things will look drastically different when I get out and the Fourth of July rolls around because it won't be my dad manning the pit — it will be my brother. It won't be my mom in the kitchen whipping up the homemade potato salad — it will be my sister. Although I've lost both parents during my incarceration, the family love and unity will still clearly be present.

Initially I was a bit reluctant to write this blog entry because I, in no way, wanted to detract from the essence and spirit of what Independence Day *truly* represents. Without question, I appreciate what every serviceman and woman has done, and continues to do, for this country and our freedom as American citizens. But I would also be remiss if I commemorated the freedoms of this country without highlighting the lack of freedom for over two million of her citizens. Granted, we put ourselves here by violating the law, and I am in no way asking for sympathy or pity — that's not my point. I merely want to underscore the fact that as we in prison go through yet another holiday without the comfort, familiarity, and bonding with friends and family, it's a bit difficult to celebrate the essence of independence.

Therefore, even as I wish all of you who are reading this a wonderful holiday where you can enjoy great food and fun with friends and family, I know a part of you will be incomplete as you miss your incarcerated loved one. We on the inside, obviously, will, likewise, be missing our loved ones even more so on this holiday as well. Nonetheless, I'd like to wish you all a happy Independence Day! As for myself and over two million others in my position, we will continue to long for and eagerly await our own day of independence.

FDA DISAPPROVED

My stomach growled around 4:30 p.m. and all I could do was think about dinner and how I was going to devour it the minute I sat down with my tray of food. I didn't even bother to look at the menu ahead of time to see what they would be serving us tonight — I was so hungry it didn't matter.

The bell rang moments later, and I sprang from my cell when my door opened. I strolled into the semi-packed dining hall — the tables and seats segregated by race and gang — and instinctively glanced at people's trays on their tables to see what the fine cuisine was that I was about to feast on in a few minutes. But my eagerness quickly subsided into a lackluster anticipation of merely nourishing my body and satisfying my large appetite.

The spaghetti sauce sat in an immovable clump atop a pile of sticky noodles. It appeared to be an attempt at a meat sauce, but the meat (if we can call it that; the jury is still out as I write this) was ground so fine that it fused with the sauce into a heap of, well, your guess is as good as any.

I grabbed my tray and sidestepped through the serving line while peering to my left to see what the next inmate server offered. I found myself slightly distracted by the fact that none of them wore protective nets over their unkempt beards. That had to be a violation of some health code, right? In spite of my trepidation to continue through the line, I stopped in front of the first station, which had salad that appeared to have been sitting out a little longer (I'm being generous) than it should have. You know how half of it looks fresh, but it is interspersed with the other half that is beginning to brown and become soggier by the minute? Yes, even *that* lettuce would have been better than what I was staring at!

I bypassed the "salad" and slid down to the blatantly overcooked spaghetti noodles and reluctantly stuck my plastic tray underneath the metal partition that separated the servers from the rest of us. The tall, dark-haired, unenthusiastic server dipped his plastic bowl into the large metal pan that held the contents I was set to receive and came up with a solid pile of paleness that he plopped onto the center of my tray. I instinctively made a wry expression as I felt my stomach turn at the thought of digesting this, but I continued down the line anyway.

Next was the meat sauce. The stubborn paste was served from a large ladle, but before the server poured it over my noodles I could see the layer of orange grease that defiantly refused to mesh with the "meat" that shared its vicinity.

After receiving the sauce, I quickly stuck my tray in to receive the French bread. French bread is usually pretty good. But – forgive me if I'm mistaken – isn't French bread supposed to be thick and toasted but still somewhat soft when you squeeze it? Well, let's just say this bread must have been on the Miami Beach diet and was about as soft as a bowling ball! Oh well, so much for expecting French bread to be French bread.

Dessert — there's no way to mess that up, right? The chocolate chip "congo" bar (a square, cookie-like dessert) was pried from a grease-laden pan and dropped onto my tray with a resounding thud. When I picked it up to take a bite, my fingers were left greasier than they would have been had I changed the oil in my car myself.

But I ate. I consumed each bite of my food with the sole purpose of replenishing the nutrients I had expended throughout the day.

My point in illustrating (admittedly with a hint of hyperbole) what a typical prison meal looks like is to underscore the importance of appreciating how blessed those of you not in prison are to be able to pick and choose what you want to eat. Granted, prior to prison I was the first to complain about my McDonald's burger having a soggy tomato or my fries not being piping hot. I'd complain about having to eat either chicken or pork chops every other day because that's what my then-girlfriend found to be the quickest things to make for dinner.

But having now been exposed to this mass-productively-cooked food, what I wouldn't give now for some of those lukewarm fries or routine pork chops! Suffice it to say, I won't be complaining much about food when this is over.

TIME TO SPREAD

The steel table designed to seat four is placed in the middle of the dayroom, piled with snack food: assorted bags of chips, several bags of refried beans, white rice, many summer sausages, tubs of cheese spread, blocks of cheddar cheese, packages of cookies, donuts, juice packs, and much more that no one on a diet should come within a hundred feet of. It must be someone's birthday!

No doubt, most (if not all) of you have heard your incarcerated loved one rave about how good and tasty their jailhouse burritos and nachos are. The jailhouse spread has unequivocally become a staple in prisons and jails everywhere across the country. It is a way for us to treat ourselves for someone's birthday or holidays such as Christmas and Thanksgiving. I never thought my taste buds would evolve enough to enjoy the "exotic" flavors produced by a jailhouse spread — but they did!

The typical nacho spread is composed of the following ingredients and made in the following manner: Hot water (190 degrees) is added to the dried refried beans and sit to cook in a container for a few minutes. Summer sausages are cut up into small cubes using a ruler. White (or brown, if you prefer) rice is cooked the same way as the beans are and sit (without stirring) for several minutes until done. Chips are then carefully laid across the plastic trays (technically designed to serve as a pencil holder, but it works all the same) and the beans are poured across the chips. The rice is layered next, and more beans are laid on top of the rice. The next layer is the diced meat, followed by the thin, creamy cheese spread. Lastly, the block cheese is diced up and sprinkled across the top layer to complete the "fine cuisine."

Guys gleefully dig in, filling themselves until they are physically unable to stomach another bite. We socialize and celebrate the occasion around this meal with the same jubilation (okay, *almost* the same) we would if we were celebrating a special occasion with friends in the free world.

When I first described this meal to my loved ones over the phone, I could hear them cringe at the thought of eating something like this — voluntarily, no less. I tried my best to convince them to see it from my vantage point, but that just wasn't going to happen. Viewing it from their perspective, I believe I'd probably instinctively gag too if they were describing how they had put all those random ingredients together into one dish.

But my family and fiancée know that these meals mean something to me; that they are not simply desirable because of the acquired taste I've developed for them, but rather they are all we have to commemorate special occasions in this very limited setting. Birthdays are still important to inmates, obviously, and besides the desire to receive cards from loved ones wishing us a happy birthday, we look forward to spreading with our friends in celebration. The jailhouse spread is our version of going out to our favorite local restaurant with neighborhood friends to celebrate our birthday.

It still amazes me how innovative inmates can be; how we are able to adapt to our environment and create as normal a life as possible for however long we are confined. This is why I can be excited about the prospect of eating a jailhouse spread for someone's birthday, while my family and loved ones (and likely ninety percent of the general public) wouldn't eat it for any amount of money!

Ahhh... the infamous jailhouse spread. No doubt, this is perhaps the most common, simple pleasure of prison life across America. It is a great meal for many of us who have grown unaccustomed to eating fresh food that is available to those in society, but it is also much more than that; it is a meaningful way for us to come together and create a sense of humanity and celebration when we need it the most.

WHERE ARE THEY NOW?

Prior to coming to prison, my circle of friends consisted of the same small group of guys from my childhood. We went to school together, hung out after school, and virtually spent all our waking hours together.

As adults, we each lived with our "primary" girlfriends, held solid jobs and would get together on weekends to catch up and have fun. Our friendship, in my opinion, was as solid as a group's could be.

When I was arrested, I'd call home (to my parents' home) and, sure enough, my friends would be there with my brother, so I was able to talk to them. They even came to visit me a few times while I was in the county jail — which was located only twenty minutes away. This was exactly what I had hoped for and expected from the guys I considered family when my incarceration started.

Nearly a year later I was sentenced to seventeen-and-a-half years. When I'd call my friends at their respective homes, however, the phone calls were being accepted less and less. The visits became more spaced out until they ceased altogether. From time to time my brother would tell me that so-and-so said to tell me, "What's up?" or "Keep your head up." But I wanted to hear these things from them directly, not through my brother. Sadly, direct support from my friends became non-existent.

The lack of support from the people who had always been my closest allies hurt me beyond what I thought was possible. I have continually pondered this and struggled with how I "should" feel about them since this has happened. They, technically, don't owe me anything; after all, I put myself here. They are not obligated to sacrifice anything to show me their loyalty or support. Yet, even though my rational mind tells me these things and accepts them as true, my emotional self (in other words, my heart) tells me this is wrong. My feelings tell me this is not reflective of a *real* friendship and that I *am* justified in feeling slighted and upset with how things have unfolded between us.

This reality is, sadly, a very common outcome for many who find themselves in this situation. It is a complete anomaly (in my experience) if, and when, someone in prison maintains regular contact with their group of closest friends throughout their sentence. Many of us, however, accept the fact that perhaps many of these people were not our loyal friends after all — or were they? Could it be they do love us but are simply too busy with life to the point that time has gotten away from them, and before they knew it years had gone by? I don't know, but this doesn't seem so farfetched in my opinion. Again, I don't have a "good" answer that would make me feel okay with this result. This is my conflict. On one hand, I'm hurt that my closest friends have acted as though I no longer exist — as if I'm dead. On the other hand, I sympathize with their position because they did not send me to prison, and they have their own busy lives to maintain. I'm just hurt. I'm conflicted as to how I ought to feel about this. I really miss my friends. I wish they were here. Where are they?

A RAINBOW AWAITS

I'm not sure about you, but I don't particularly like the rain. In fact, it makes me just want to stay indoors, drink a large cup of coffee with lots of creamer and Splenda® sweetener, and watch TV or read an enjoyable book. It appears the rain generally casts a downtrodden mood across mankind. But what we fail to envision during a torrential downpour is the bright, beautiful rainbow that often emerges in its aftermath.

Prison is by no means a fun, uplifting, wholesome place. Many of you hear from your loved ones just how tense, violent, degrading, and dehumanizing this experience can be. Yet, for many of us, this experience has also been a pivotal turning point in our lives that has enabled us to truly discover ourselves, passions, talents, and ultimately our purpose in life. We have been able to develop our physical, mental, and spiritual selves perhaps more than ever before. In essence, prison has saved many of us from ourselves and given us a greater quality of life than we would have likely had if we had we not come here.

This experience — like rainy days — does not inherently put us in a good mood and bring the best out of us as the sun can often do. But prison does offer a beautiful reward at the end of it. For many of us, this will come in the form of a greater appreciation for relationships with our family, girlfriends/wives, and children, a clean and sober lifestyle, a formal education, and an ability to maintain healthy relationships with people while enjoying a life that is devoid of continual chaos and self-inflicted pain.

Keeping this proverbial vision in my mind of a bright, radiant rainbow that surely awaits me at the end of my "storm" helps me stay focused and optimistic about my life now and hereafter. Like anyone else, I have my down days, but I know that had I not come to prison, my life would have, no doubt, been an endless cycle of addiction, pain, emptiness, and self-destruction. When I'm brutally honest with myself, I should, in a weird way, be thankful for prison. Not because it's an ideal, warm and fuzzy place to be, obviously, but because of the growth it has spurred in me and the accomplishments I have attained as a result.

In the same way that we marvel at an immaculate, radiant rainbow that appears after a dreary day of rain gives way to a beaming sun, we ought to understand and appreciate the profound quality of life that awaits many of us once our sentence is up. The same way it is necessary that rain *must* come before the rainbow, so it is that those of us who are incarcerated must endure a challenging situation to bring about a dramatic change in our lives that will lead to a beautiful future. When I came to this realization was when I began to focus on my own rainbow that inevitably awaits me, so I encourage you to remind your incarcerated loved one(s) of this analogy when you sense they could use a word of encouragement the most.

A MOMENT OF HUMANITY

It's anything but breaking news to announce that prison is, in large part, a place designed to dehumanize, degrade, and mentally debilitate its occupants. The treatment of being disrespected by prison staff without provocation is routine – many assuming an inmate is innately deviant and pathologically manipulative. Being made to feel like your state identification number is more important than your name is to be expected from most prison staff.

I like to think of myself as a strong-minded man who can easily insulate himself from the dehumanizing nature of prison, but even I have my moments where I allow it to affect me. When the negative, unprovoked belittlement by prison staff is so pervasive and continuous, it's not hard to understand how even the most mentally temperate inmate can be affected psychologically. Having said that, however, I'll also be the first to admit that not *all* prison staff treats inmates this way. Just like not *all* of *any* demographic (even inmates) or group behave the same way simply because they share certain characteristics.

In the context of understanding how negatively prison can affect one's sense of self-worth and self-esteem, I wanted to share what happened at work today.

Since transferring to this prison only two and a half months ago, I've been working at the DMV call center located within the prison. Several civilian DMV employees manage the call center, and there are about twenty-five inmate call agents who field calls from the public to answer their DMV-related questions. The work environment is professional — just as you'd expect from most call centers.

The workday started in a typical fashion. Everyone went to their respective cubicles, set up their computer screens and settings, put on their headsets, and began answering the onslaught of incoming calls that awaited us. When lunchtime rolled around, however, I experienced what turned out to be my first humane experience since arriving here.

We were led into a huge area where barbecue burgers, hot dogs, and other food you'd expect at a barbecue awaited us. We gleefully filled our paper plates with all the food, took our seats, and delved into the delicious assortment of food. After we ate, an inmate camera man entered the room and asked us if we wanted our pictures taken in our work area so our loved ones could see us in our work environment. Men excitedly lined up for this rare opportunity. We casually talked, ate, took pictures with each other, and enjoyed the spirit of the occasion — oh, did I fail to mention what the occasion was?

I learned that the DMV contractors that do business with the Department of Corrections orchestrated this day of appreciation for their workers. Wait, did you get that? I said *they* appreciate *us*! This is not something they had to do. They'd still get the same level of productivity out of their inmate workers whether they rewarded us in this way or not. Realizing this, it gave me a sense of humanity in a situation that deprives us of this quality daily. As I took every bite of my food, I thought of this. I enjoyed every bit of the perfectly grilled food but will savor the *meaning* of the food much longer. One can truly become desensitized to being treated inhumanely when it has been the norm for so many years, but it is days like today that starkly remind me I am still human and deserve to be treated as such. The food was great, but the moment of humanity I felt was invaluable.

THE STREETS DON'T LOVE YOU

I cannot tell you how many inmates I've met and have conversed with who have expressed their disdain and indignation for the lack of support they've received from their "friends" and "homies" from the streets since they've been in prison. They are shocked and dismayed to discover people they had always thought loved them and would do anything for them are nowhere to be found once the dust has settled and they are confined to a six-by-nine-foot cell for years. No letters. No accepted collect calls. No money. Nothing. But think about it: these so-called friends are guys who, for the most part, have made a life of committing crime themselves, manipulating others to do things for them, and living by a model that puts self above everyone else.

The friends I speak of are not wholesome, childhood friends whose friendships are based on values and principles that are upright; I'm referring to the bonds built with those who dwell in the streets and live by a code of conduct that runs contrary to societal standards and expectations. These friendships are typically, although not exclusively, found within the gang culture.

Many men in prison, as you can imagine, belong to gangs. They operate from the notion that their loyalty to their gang supersedes that even to their biological family. Members of their gang, they believe, are the guys who "have their back" and "look out for them" at all cost. Yet, when these young men find themselves in prison, the loyalty they thought was embedded in their bonds with their street friends that would surely show up when they needed it the most is nowhere to be found. Consequently, they logically begin to question if what they have devoted their lives to and ultimately sacrificed their freedom for was worth it. They quickly become disillusioned with the idea of belonging to a group of friends who, when they needed them, were nowhere to be found. This doesn't reflect loyalty, solidarity, or commitment. Yet, these were exactly the principles they were told they were buying into when being recruited and pledging their loyalty to the gang. What was used to recruit them turned out to be a false promise, an enticing lie that revealed itself when it was put to the test.

It is not their friends from the streets who are there, supporting them through this most difficult circumstance — it is their real family. It's Mom. It's Dad. It's their brother, sister, grandparents and other family members. It's not "Big Mike" or "Flaco" walking through the door to greet them when they enter the visiting room . . . it's their family. It's not "Lil' Gunsmoke" or "Spider" sending birthday and Christmas cards, it's Grandma and Grandpa, Mom and Dad. It's ironic that these young men would forsake their family to join a gang in the streets, creating a pseudo-family they believe will love them as a real family would, only to discover it was not the band of "brothers" they pledged their loyalty to who would support them in their time of need — but their family, the one they chose to forsake for their gang.

I used gangs as my focal point of reference here because it's a common theme in this situation, but it doesn't have to be a gang that reveals this truism; it can be any network of people you befriend and share important ties with who disappear when you need them most. Generally, street ties are not rooted in principles that would comprise a genuine friendship based on love, loyalty, and support. No. They are characterized by superficiality, selfishness, and manipulation. Sadly, these young men don't realize this until it's too late. That's why I make it a point during my conversations with them to tell them, "The streets don't love you . . . they just take you away from people who do."

DEFYING THE ODDS

We all encounter life's most arduous circumstances from different vantage points and with varying levels of support to help us through them. We also are differentially equipped to cope with and overcome such trials with a renewed sense of perspective on life. What I've noticed in my experience and many others' in this circumstance is a common thread of human might and a defiant will and determination to turn one's gravest misfortune into a profound sense of purpose and triumph.

In the beginning of any painful loss is immense grief and a sense of chaos and helplessness. But as humans, we have the uncanny ability to adapt to even the most extreme adversity. We notice that as we begin to accept what is and turn our attention to how we can gain the most out of the situation before us, we are greeted with strength we didn't even know we possessed. Our sense of helplessness metamorphoses into an invigorated sense of empowerment and control over our destiny.

In my experience, the most distinguishing characteristic that separates those who thrive in times of immense adversity (such as prison) and those who succumb to their plight is belief. Belief in oneself and the ability to overcome is the essential ingredient to success that comes out of many tragic situations. The biggest hurdle for those incarcerated, however, is having enough positive people in their corner to counter the pervasive negativity that surrounds them. It seems for every person who speaks encouragement, there are ten who spew the opposite. But belief in oneself is cultivated, not inherent. It is built over time and through trials; it is not instantaneous. When it takes root, and begins to drive our thoughts, actions, behavior and habits, then our character and destiny become much more defined and sustainable.

Many of us in prison have lived our lives doing the opposite of what society, our parents, and our communities would have liked for us to do. As a result, we have been labeled as "bad," "criminal," and "no good." When we internalized these beliefs, our behavior quickly followed suit because, well, if everyone says these things about us, we reasoned, they must be true! Now we find ourselves in this dreaded situation and we are again treated by staff in the prisons and even family members like we are still "worthless" or "no good," and told that we'll never amount to anything — no matter how hard we try! We again believe these things and subsequently are released from prison only to return within a year or two because we *believe* we can never change, that we can never be anything but bad. Statistics show this to be true.

Those leaving prison face discrimination at every turn: employment, housing, insurance, etc. We are more likely to return to prison than someone who has never been to prison. In other words, as the old saying goes, the odds are stacked against us. For many, this is intimidating enough to throw in the towel and resign themselves to the falsehood that no matter how hard they try, things will never change for them. Well, many *have* in fact defied those odds.

Defying these daunting odds starts with a mindset, a mentality rooted in non-negotiable self-determination and perseverance. I've found prison to be a suitable place to transform one's life because of the lack of distraction (drugs, alcohol, familiar places and people, etc.) and time to self-reflect. It certainly gives a person reason enough to examine his or her life's decisions and contemplate what he or she could have done differently in many instances to bring about more desirable results. And with the support of wonderful, loving people like you and many others out there, how can one *not* succeed? Defying the odds is not easy, but then again what is?

FRIENDS IN LOW PLACES

I recently received a letter from a pen pal discussing some of the publicly held views surrounding what prison is and isn't. We'd been discussing some of the many myths that abound, and I'd been doing my best in our first three or four letters to dispel some of the misconceptions she had regarding prison culture and customs. I'm obviously aware of the pervasive stereotypes and how prisons and prisoners are portrayed in shows like "Lock Up" and others. But it was in my pen pal's last letter where something was asserted that struck a chord with me like nothing had prior to that point. To paraphrase, she said she didn't believe "real friendships" were possible in a prison setting.

My pen pal (by the way, I have discussed my sentiments with her already) was making the drastic mistake that many people do regarding the ability of prisoners to form genuine friendships. They categorize many inmates as so unscrupulous and deceitful that those they don't believe fall into that category must remain vigilant to the point of insulation and isolation from forming close bonds with our peers. Although I understand the rationale of this position, it's simply not true.

When I came to prison over eleven years ago, it didn't take long before I found myself routinely walking to chow, eating meals, lifting weights, and engaging in other leisurely activities with the same individuals. This is a natural occurrence, as you can imagine, in a social environment of any kind. These weren't necessarily "friendships" in those instances; they were people I socialized with, to get along with those in my immediate surroundings, and adapt to my new living situation. Over the years, however, after spending a lot of time with some of these same individuals (and others), genuine friendships did develop.

When my father died, I turned to my fiancée and family for comfort. But that was only after the almost immediate embrace I received from my cellmate who, upon my entrance of the cell after being told the news, asked me what was wrong. I told him in an almost inaudible voice that I'd lost my dad. He stood up from the stool he was sitting on, extended his arms, and hugged me. There we were, embracing, while I literally cried on this man's shoulders. The irony of two "criminals" embracing in a compassionate moment did not set upon me in that instant — the humanity did.

I have been fortunate to have met and befriended several genuine friends in prison who I can wholeheartedly confide in and trust with any information, and they have that same level of confidence in me. The principles of a friendship don't change simply because we are in prison. Self-disclosure, support, reliance, and mutuality make up friendships in here just as they do out there. People who have made mistakes by breaking the law and subsequently being sent to prison do not suddenly become incapable of forming substantive bonds with other people in their circumstance merely because of where they are.

I don't make this case under the pretense of believing I can convince anyone who reads this that prison is a jolly-go-lucky place where all its occupants spend each day in harmony and friendly interaction — I know better! That would be ridiculous and foolhardy on my part. Certainly, there are manipulative, cunning, deceitful people here who cannot be trusted with anything! But is this simply because they're in prison, or is it more reflective of their character that — albeit likely had something to do with them coming to prison — has rendered them unlikely to form close bonds with people in general, despite where they are? Are these types of people not roaming the streets and in office buildings in every city in America?

Friendships are a human necessity. They enable us to get through the worst situations life throws at us. They provide a sense of security, comfort, and reason when we need them the most. Inmates are no different. Granted, we are not surrounded by common-day Gandhis and Martin Luther Kings, but who is? The fact of the matter is, despite what we've done, we are human and therefore rely on the same type of close bonds as people do anywhere else in the world. The only difference is we do it behind bars.

FALLING INTO PLACE

When I came to prison over twelve years ago, I felt like my life was over! I was 24 years old and facing twenty years in prison. When the officer placed those cold, steel handcuffs on my wrists, I saw a lifetime of dreams, hopes, and memories instantly fade into oblivion – for they had vanished in that fateful moment.

As time went on, however, and the initial shock began to wane and acceptance set in, I felt a newfound sense of relief that I could handle this; that contrary to my initial thoughts of doom and gloom for the foreseeable future, this wasn't the absolute worse situation I could be in. And instead of focusing on what I *didn't* have, I chose to put my focus on what I *did* have, which was my health, family, sanity, and general well-being. This gave me a sense of hope and stability during my darkest hour.

While serving this sentence, I've been fortunate enough to be able to pursue a higher education. I could, without distraction, reassess my life and what I want to do with it; to explore what I want to do for a career – something that would add meaning and purpose to my life, which is something I had never earnestly thought about prior to prison. As a result, I have discovered my life's passion and purpose that I didn't even know I had. I've found a sense of direction and a clearly defined path while in a confined setting. It appears to me that my incarceration was necessary to bring about a keen sense of awareness, self-discovery, and a focus on my future that I'd not known before. Of course, in the beginning, I could not see this at all, not even a little bit. All that I could see and feel were despair and sorrow over what I had made of my life and the havoc I wreaked in others' lives.

MY PRISON LIFE

When we envision ourselves leading a certain life and living out our dreams and goals, then it all goes awry in an instant and we're left scrambling to make sense of it, we are left with nothing to believe other than our lives have fallen apart. Everything we had hoped for is now gone. But if we leave ourselves open to learn, grow, and self-reflect in these moments of extreme turmoil, we do ourselves a service that will have an impact for a lifetime. It is in those moments that we are compelled to analyze our past thoughts, behaviors, and motives. Why did we think certain things, do certain things, and conduct ourselves in these ways for so many years? We are able to honestly assess these areas of our lives and piece together why and how we ended up where we are when we commit ourselves to this process. It is only here that we come to a place of enlightenment and, hopefully, motivation to change our foundational thought processes, ambitions, and the overall trajectory of our lives.

Regardless of what you believe in terms of spirituality, philosophy, or simply why things happen the way they do, it is irrefutable that humans have invariably found meaning and purpose in their most adverse circumstances. It is here that we find a reason to search ourselves internally for something greater, something deeper, even if we don't know what we're looking for. But what usually happens is we end up surprising ourselves with what we find, and it adds immeasurable substance and fulfillment to our lives. The outcome is far different than what we perceived when our lives became in disarray and seemed to be falling apart.

Perhaps we can't make sense of everything that happens in our lives, especially when something like prison happens and impacts children, wives, parents, and families of all kinds in immeasurable ways. All we see initially is the fact that our loved ones are unreachable and will be for many years in most cases. But if we are not careful and vigilant, we'll miss the primary lesson and purpose that we are to take from it – both the incarcerated and the free. We all stand to learn from adversity; it's up to us *what* we learn and to what extent that learning will be. The key thing to remember through it all, though, is when disaster strikes and all of a sudden life becomes chaotic beyond comprehension, our lives are usually not falling apart – they're merely falling into place.

INMATE HEALTHCARE

I'm sure you all have an inkling of how the healthcare system works in prison. For many, I'd imagine that you envision inattentive health care providers who spend more time staring down at their clipboard than paying attention to the inmate in front of them who is informing them of their ailments. Perhaps some of you picture long lines of inmates in the waiting area for hours only to be told by the receptionist that the lone doctor's remaining appointments for the day have been cancelled, thus they must be rescheduled and return to their cells in the same dismal state they entered the medical facility. Indeed, I suspect these scenarios are ubiquitous across the nation's many jails and prisons – but that hasn't been my experience.

The Oregon Department of Corrections has its flaws and shortcomings like any system that is responsible for taking care of thousands of people in every conceivable way for their survival. But in my twelve and a half years of being incarcerated, I have only had satisfactory experiences with the healthcare provided, receiving treatment for *everything* that has ailed me – medically and dentally related. Let me explain how it generally works.

When you feel an unusual pain or ailment of any kind that you know should not be there, you must go to the officer's station, grab a "medical kyte" to fill out, put it in the medical box on your way to the dining hall, and wait for a response. Generally, within two to three days the kyte will come back to you with medical's response. Usually it will say you've been scheduled for Sick Call, which is where everyone who has a medical issue will be seen by a nurse to assess whether, or not, they need to be referred to the doctor for further evaluation. Sick Call usually occurs within a day or two, and as I just mentioned, the nurse will listen to your issue and, in most cases, refer you to a doctor.

MY PRISON LIFE

We each have an assigned doctor based on the first letter of our last name. In my experience, there has generally been one doctor per 300 - 400 inmates. Granted, this doesn't sound very reassuring, but you also should remember that many people (especially men) don't see the doctor unless they're on their deathbed, so that number is drastically reduced in practical terms.

In most cases, the proper medication is prescribed, and you'll be scheduled again several weeks later to be re-evaluated. If the problem persists, a new medication is prescribed, and the process continues. If what afflicts you is beyond their ability to resolve or something that requires surgery, the doctor will refer you to a specialist (outside the prison).

Inmates can be put on a regular (quarterly or semi-annually) schedule, if they request, to have their blood drawn for lab testing, just to make sure everything is normal and there's no cause for concern. Medications are always prescribed for a year at a time; when it needs to be renewed, you simply fill out a kyte (inmate communication form), put it in the medical box, and it is returned days later with a stamp that says "RENEWED."

I don't pretend, however, to paint my experience as the status quo for all or even most inmates. We all have unique needs and therefore will receive varying levels of attention. What I can say is that compared to what I've seen on television and read in articles and newspapers about healthcare in other prison systems, Oregon is leaps and bounds above many others. Sure, I've witnessed inmates who clearly needed a major surgery for years only to be denied and stalled until their release. I've also seen inmates receive surgery but little to no follow-up physical therapy or instruction on how they can best aid their recovery themselves. I will concede that these instances can only be construed as neglectful; but when countless others in our shoes can't even get blood pressure or cholesterol medication, I'm not going to complain about not having access to physical therapy after a needed surgery.

It is nothing short of a blessing to have access to medical and dental care (at no cost to us) while incarcerated. Many people take these provisions for granted, but I know there are still millions of American citizens who are without healthcare, even after the implementation of the historical Affordable Care Act. As a prisoner who will have a hard road ahead as a "branded" member of society, I am grateful for at least having my most basic health care needs met while here.

PART II

Maximizing Your Potential Behind Bars

MY ROCK BOTTOM

It was a frigid Tuesday morning in January when I arrived at the state prison located in eastern Oregon. I went through the intake process where I was dressed in blue jeans, T-shirt, and state-issued black canvass shoes. I was a helpless, hopeless, twenty-five-year-old looking at spending the next seventeen-and-a-half years in this awful place.

The next day, along with everyone else, I exited the packed dorm in a hurried frenzy when "yard line" blared over the unit's PA system. As I walked around the large track, I surveyed my new surroundings. Guys vigorously lifted weights while others intensely played basketball or horseshoes. Other inmates walked in pairs around the track while discussing their thin hopes for an appeal or bemoaned how their relationships with girlfriends/wives were deteriorating with each passing day.

The thought of a monotonous, day-in, day-out, year-after-year empty existence for the next seventeen years depressed me. I couldn't fathom having my young life waste away in this fashion. With each passing lap around the track on that frigid winter day, I began to assess how my life ended up this way and, most importantly, what I was going to do about it. I decided it was imperative that I pick apart my life, particularly focusing on my patterns of behavior, faulty thought processes, insecurities, and other character defects that were at the root of my alcoholism and destructive decision making. I decided I would spend the next seventeen years undertaking this huge endeavor. I understood the gravity of the moment; I'd finally hit the lowest, most vulnerable point of my life that demanded I do a thorough assessment of my shortcomings and make a commitment to bettering myself in those areas.

I determined in that two hours I spent walking the track to diligently commit myself to working on my flaws, one by one, so I would emerge from prison a healthy, proud, intelligent, mature man that society and my family could respect. I knew it wouldn't be easy — not by any stretch — but I also knew I had no other choice if I was going to salvage the rest of my life and bring meaning and purpose to my future — regardless of where I was physically.

It has now been nearly eleven years since that frigid winter day, and although I'm not perfect in eradicating all my shortcomings that I'm now aware I possess, I *am* encouraged and proud to say I'm far from the young, selfish, insecure kid who entered prison eleven years ago.

I've also asked family and friends to hold me accountable when I exhibit some of these undesirable behaviors. I readily admit that I couldn't have developed in the way I have if I had not had their unrelenting support along the way. After all, they are an essential part of my motivation for wanting to evolve into the best version of Martin I can be. I'm not where I want to be in terms of overcoming all my character defects, but I'm certainly not where I was! And I've learned the key to my success is to not allow myself to become complacent in this effort. My growth will need to be continuous — lasting a lifetime. For anyone, this should be true, but it usually takes a remarkable moment of clarity to reveal the necessity of making such a commitment. Psychologists have coined several terms in reference to this mentality, but in laymen's terms, we simply call it rock bottom.

NO MORE EXCUSES!

Have you ever wondered why it is that hundreds of thousands of people in this country spend years in prison, get out, swear they'll never return, and then find themselves back in this horrid situation? If nothing else, one would think that a parolee would instantly reflect on how much they hated prison when faced with temptation to break the law, thus causing them to immediately abandon this destructive thought. Apparently, however, this *doesn't* happen because if it did, there would be little to no repeat offenders.

Sadly, I too am a repeat offender. I did all that was asked of me during my first incarceration (i.e. cognitive restructuring classes, GED completion, drug and alcohol education, and other rehabilitative classes). I was a model inmate whom others looked up to and even admired in some respects. I graduated from an early-release boot camp program as valedictorian of my platoon and was released from prison after serving a total of three years and two months. I returned to prison in less than two years with a seventeen-and-a-half-year sentence.

Having matured considerably over the last ten plus years of my incarceration, while acquiring an education that has enabled me to understand my erroneous thinking patterns, I now know exactly *why* I re-offended and why many others eventually do so as well. As much as I appeared to be leading a productive life after I'd gotten out the first time (I was working full time, attending college part time, and moving up in the company), I was never honest with myself about what had brought me to prison in the first place. The underlying issues that led to my addiction as a teenager still claimed a significant stake in my life, even as I went through the many rehabilitation classes during my first incarceration. Therefore, when I was released and began to make steps toward a better future, I irrationally allowed my moderate success to become a reason to think I can drink "a little" here and there, despite being an alcoholic. I rationalized it by telling myself, *you're okay; look how well you're doing.*

This insidious pattern of destructive thinking is unequivocally rooted in pride (not the good kind either). My untamed pride caused me to avoid being honest with myself and admitting that I wasn't, in fact, as strong as I thought, nor had I addressed my underlying issues and learned to be responsible as much as I could have. I'd convinced myself that I didn't really belong in prison in the first place, that I didn't have anything to really work on and correct. Clearly, I now know that was not the case at all!

I see and hear this type of dangerous thinking almost daily, and it actually makes sense because it's a classic defense mechanism that we *all* use. We instinctively search for ways to minimize feeling pain, guilt, or insecurity. But when it comes to criminal behavior and/or drug or alcohol addiction, the stakes are too high to use rationalization and denial as defense mechanisms.

I've learned the hard way that not being completely and brutally honest with myself about what brought me to prison the first time was exactly what brought me back for a lengthy second stint. Now I understand that my only chance to succeed in this situation — and life beyond prison — is to make no more excuses.

HOW MUCH IS TOO MUCH?

Before coming to prison, I remember reading newspaper articles and watching television and seeing people my age and younger being sentenced to five, ten, fifteen or more years for various crimes. I used to think to myself, *there's no way I could ever do that much time!* I looked at these condemned folks as if they were all dead men walking — completely severed from human contact and life as they knew it. I couldn't fathom being in their shoes a single day — let alone years.

While sitting in the county jail facing nearly twenty years at the age of twenty-four, I still could not fathom in my wildest nightmare being sentenced to that amount of time. I thought to myself, *I'd die before I could finish a sentence that long — or go insane!*

It's almost impossible to grasp and appreciate how much hardship we are capable of enduring until we are forced to navigate very arduous circumstances. It is merely the exposure to challenging circumstances that elicits the response needed to surmount such obstacles. Although I'd spent just over three years in prison on a prior offense, I still had no concept of what it would take to live a life of confinement and physical isolation from my friends and family for this long a time. But when I was thrust into this life with no choice in the matter, obviously, I did what most people do — adapt.

As humans, we don't give ourselves enough credit as to how capable we are of adapting to and conquering unforeseen, seemingly insurmountable obstacles. I have no doubt that just as you are reading this, you're thinking to yourself, *there's no way I could survive in prison for years — no way!* Believe me, I understand your sentiment. God forbid you'd ever have to find out what your response to this situation would be, but I can almost promise that no matter what hardships you are afflicted with in this life, you *do* find a way to adapt, overcome, and move on. You'll mentally accept your misfortune (after much sorrow, pain, bargaining, and anger) and settle in to the reality that is. Your brain will then search for ways to reassess your situation, which will enable you to decrease your stress level and acclimate to the circumstance. You'll create new expectations, inevitably changing the things you look forward to and get excited about.

I read a book (*The Pursuit of Happiness*) a while ago that illustrated the remarkable ability and inevitability for humans to adapt to extreme adversity. In a follow-up interview with two men — a paraplegic who was injured in a car accident and a multi-million-dollar lottery winner — who both went through their respective life-altering events six months prior to the interview, each man was asked to report his level of happiness at that time. Astonishingly, both men reported having the *same* level of happiness! How can this be? It has been discovered that our brains experience a "jolt" of energy and euphoria when something really exciting or novel happens, but over time — no matter how thrilling or bad it is — our brain settles down to a normal level of chemical activity. The novelty wears off, we adapt to our new circumstance, and we feel "normal" again. This extraordinary illustration can be summed up in my life's motto: life is ten percent what happens to you and ninety percent how you react to it. It also reaffirmed to me that we are inherently creatures of adaptation. Simply put, we invariably find ways to adapt to and thrive in any situation after the initial shock has subsided.

I WILL NOT BECOME "INSTITUTIONALIZED"

The American Heritage dictionary defines institutionalized as follows: "To [confine] in an institution." Clearly, this has already taken place in my life and has been the case for over ten years now. But there is a stark difference between being physically confined in a prison and conforming one's psyche and behavior to the point where one views a situation as a normal existence. Put more simply, I refuse to accept physical captivity as normal or acceptable. However, there are many inmates who conform so extensively to this oppressive form of living that they are, sadly, unable to properly function in society when they are eventually released; thus, the culture shock they experience when they get out becomes so distressing that they rapidly spiral back into destructive — often illegal — behavior that lands them back in prison where they're, frankly, more comfortable.

The acceptance of prison life is essential for any of us to get through our sentence as comfortably as possible. Obviously, it behooves one in this predicament to not try to buck the system by refusing to comply with the rules of prison, but this level of conformity is not what I mean when I speak of becoming "institutionalized."

I have seen this insidious transformation occur especially in younger inmates coming into the system and not knowing what to expect. They will often quickly link up with a prison gang for protection. From that point on they become immersed and indoctrinated into the prison culture of violence, deceit, manipulation, defiance, and contempt for authority figures. This assertion is not to claim that these characteristics didn't already exist to a degree within these individuals, but in my experience, I have seen many young, impressionable men metamorphose right before my eyes in a matter of months. Before I knew it, these young men became unrecognizable in their speech, behavior, and attitude.

I've been cognizant and even cautious with how I refer to parts of my life here so I don't become too comfortable with this existence. For instance, many inmates refer to their cells as their "house" or our canteen as "the store," as if they were going to Safeway or a local convenience store. In my opinion, these seemingly innocuous references normalize this situation, which can subtly aid the process of becoming institutionalized. I refuse to refer to anything here with the same names I'd use outside these walls for that very reason. Prison is anything but normal.

Having said this, I can honestly say that merely referring to my cell as my house would not be an indication that I have become institutionalized to the point that I wouldn't know how to readjust to life when I'm released. We all will adjust to life in prison a little differently, all of us using various psychological strategies to cope. For those who opt to make prison feel as close to home-life as possible by ascribing familiar terms to aspects of prison life, who am I to judge? But for me personally, I refuse to do so because I have witnessed the irreparable psychological damage of becoming "too comfortable" in these surroundings.

After adopting this setting as normal and conforming to its antisocial, self-destructive culture, it's not very easy to quickly and readily readjust one's thought processes immediately upon release. Conditioning is always a process. It's not like people can simply "flip a switch" in their brains to turn off everything they've learned and conformed to through their many years in prison as soon as they return to society where there's an entirely separate set of rules and expectations. If only it were that easy.

Prison, I've learned, can be a prime opportunity to self-reflect, self-correct, and prepare to salvage a productive life when released. Conversely, it can also be a place that institutionalizes and permanently damages people's psyches, rendering them unfit to function in a free society forever more. Personally, I proudly and defiantly choose the former.

FEED WHAT FEEDS YOU

The only way for a living organism to grow and thrive in a healthy manner is to consume the proper nutrients and be nourished in a way that is conducive to its development. Our interests in life likewise follow this principle — they only reach their fullest potential with our devoted time, energy, and effort. We tend to allocate our daily time to things and people that are most important to us.

There are many things we enjoy and spend plenty of time doing throughout the day such as watching TV, reading, exercising — yes, some people find it enjoyable — and much more. But then there are other things that take on a much deeper meaning in our lives, things that fill us with incomparable joy and peace. For me, these things tend to always come in the form of helping others and making my fiancée happy. These efforts bring nourishment to my soul and fill my spirit with abundant joy and satisfaction. Therefore, I make it my personal mission to not become complacent by devoting ample time to developing these very important aspects of my life.

Regarding my relationship, it makes my heart smile when I know I've done something that makes *her* smile. I consider her feelings when making decisions. I spontaneously send her hand-drawn cards with sentimental messages because it's important that I express my love in every viable way, especially in this limiting circumstance. These are merely a few examples of how I've been able to feed what has fed me through these pivotal, life-changing years.

When it comes to mentoring others, I can say that blogging has added to my sense of purpose. Knowing that some of you are encouraged and inspired by what I write means more to me than I can express. Moreover, conducting my life in a way that causes other young men to take notice and become curious as to how I can consistently avoid the prison drama and stay focused on bettering myself has been extremely encouraging; it has even inspired some of them to do the same. Having meaningful conversations with young men who share a similar background and assuring them of their ability and potential is immeasurably rewarding. My soul leaps for joy when I am afforded these opportunities.

I imagine as life progresses, I will continue to discover more things about myself that also bring me enormous satisfaction, and when they do I will not hesitate to give them the attention and devotion they deserve, just as I have with the things I'm currently passionate about and devoted to.

I have learned that to see things grow to their fullest potential, we must give them the proper attention and "food" necessary for their growth. "Food" can come in many different forms. This principle has most certainly shown to be true in my life. Without question, the more I feed the things that matter the most, the more they reciprocally feed me.

NAVIGATE THE JUNGLE

The Amazon Rain Forest is responsible for harboring approximately fifty percent of the world's species. I imagine it to be a truly marvelous, captivating place to see and experience. On the surface it is nothing short of a zoologist's dream "laboratory" for study, and the most memorable of any tourist's South American vacation. As remarkable as this landmark habitat is, however, it is also rife with some of the world's most dangerous, venomous creatures.

Many people have asked me how I have managed to steer clear of the perpetual prison drama and negativity for so many years. I simply explain to them that prison is like a jungle — you must be mindful of and careful to steer clear of the "dangerous creatures" lurking behind and underneath the brush.

Many animals in the jungle have developed sophisticated defense mechanisms that enable them to gain an advantage over their prey while simultaneously providing protection from becoming prey themselves. For example, some harmless frogs and snakes will use mimicry as a defense mechanism by transforming their exterior colors to mimic a venomous frog or snake, thereby avoiding being attacked. Other species will camouflage themselves to blend in with their environment, enabling them to sneak up on their prey without detection. Prison is analogous to this environment.

There are many inmates who portray themselves in a nonthreatening, inviting manner, yet their underlying motive and agenda are to pounce on an unsuspecting victim whom they can take advantage of. I've witnessed this unfortunate sequence of events time and time again. Like any jungle, it's not the externally visible scenery that necessarily poses the greatest threat; it's what's lying beneath the brush and behind the trees that can cause the greatest harm.

Discernment of the true nature of your surroundings is imperative. Being vigilant and mindful of the creatures peering beneath the shrubbery from afar is a life necessity.

Any newcomer to an environment can pose a threat to the existing species in that setting. Knowing this then, it would be prudent to closely observe and learn the environment before recklessly delving in headfirst — that rarely works out. This does not mean we should live a life of paranoia and refuse to befriend anyone when we are placed in a new environment. It simply means we ought to be judicious in selecting the company we keep.

I have been as successful as I have in this situation because I've used my judgment well enough to know who, and who not, to associate with. I've managed to live in close proximity to many "creatures" who look to do harm, without becoming like them or being victimized by them, because I have stayed true to who I am and where I want to go in life. I refuse to get too close to them, because why would I voluntarily involve myself with people who represent the opposite of what I desire in life?

Life, in a sense, is like an ever-growing jungle. We will continually encounter new people, cliques, and organizations with all sorts of motives and agendas. Many people, whether in prison or not, can use manipulation to get what they want at others' expense. Because of this, it would behoove all of us to proceed through life with the vigilance and perception of a creature navigating the jungle.

STILL THANKFUL

With Thanksgiving on the horizon, there are countless inmates and their families, friends, and significant others who will predictably experience a range of emotions. For some inmates and their loved ones, this day will be extremely difficult because it will be their first Thanksgiving spent physically apart from each other. They may not know how many more they'll have to spend apart, or they do know and are dismayed and dejected at the mere thought of it. Others, on the other hand, will approach this day with a sense of joy and relief because this will represent the last Thanksgiving they must be separated; while yet others will mark this one off their calendars as one closer to being reunited with their loved ones for this cherished holiday.

We are all human and therefore vulnerable to being led or plagued by our emotions daily, especially when we are forced to be apart from those we love during times like now when we most desire to be with family. I would, nonetheless, like to offer an unconventional way of looking at this situation — one that I think can help mitigate the pain of this void.

Despite what this circumstance presents and forces us to endure, it still offers many things we ought to be thankful for. Despite the obvious fact that I must wake up in a cell every morning, I'm thankful I *can* wake up at all! I'm thankful that I have been able to recover from alcohol addiction by being here because, honestly, had this not happened, I believe I would be six feet deep in a graveyard or well on my way there.

I'm extremely thankful for the amazing woman that I met and changed my life during this pivotal, transformative phase of my life. She has been a source of continuous motivation and inspiration in helping me become the best man I can be. I'm thankful for the tremendous support I receive from friends and family who believe in what I do and encourage me to continue to vigorously pursue my goals.

I'm also thankful for having yet another opportunity at life to make the kind of impact in people's lives I always hoped to. My enthusiasm and sense of purpose have given me so much to look forward to — things I likely would have never come close to doing prior to prison.

Finally, I'm thankful to be in a place where I can eat three hot meals a day, sleep on warm blankets, shower daily with clean, hot water, and receive medical/dental care, free of charge. It's imperative that I not lose sight of how fortunate we Americans (even in prison) are in comparison to virtually any other nation on earth and those incarcerated in their prisons.

The fact undoubtedly remains that we inmates will miss our loved ones and they will deeply miss us on this Thanksgiving Day. Intense feelings of sorrow and longing are certainly valid and warranted. But I would like to challenge you to also acknowledge the many things both you and your incarcerated loved ones still should be thankful for.

DIVINE INTERVENTION

Christmas signifies many different things for people around the world. For some, it is an opportunity to congregate and spend quality time with family, generating a spirit of gratitude for having made it through another year with good health and other life blessings. For others, it represents a time of cheerful giving, selflessness, and love; and for countless kids it is a time of excitement and jubilation from receiving many gifts from family members. Whatever Christmas may mean to you personally, it is likely a special occasion.

For me, this holiday means many things, but if I am to be totally honest, it is no longer merely about spending time with family and sharing a delicious turkey dinner and exchanging gifts. Although the warm feelings we normally associate with this holiday are important, they are no longer the *most* important part of this holiday for me.

We all know the literal reason why we recognize and celebrate this holiday — to acknowledge the birth of Jesus Christ. Regardless of one's religious affiliation (or lack thereof), this is consensually and factually accepted. This is also why this time of year has taken on such a significant meaning in my life.

My faith has unquestionably been integral throughout my prison sentence and has been the catalyst that has carried me through my most difficult days in here. It has also given me a purpose through which I can base my life, as well as clarity into what avenues I am meant to pursue. It is this divine intervention during the most critical and pivotal juncture in my life that has taken me from being an alcoholic, repeat offender, to now someone who has cultivated a keen sense of and appreciation for life's most important contribution — serving others. My Lord graciously gave me a sense of calm when I felt as though no one was here with me, when I felt trapped in a whirlwind of negative, self-defeating thoughts and believed there was no positive outcome in sight. He spoke to my heart in a soothing and reassuring way that only He can.

When Christmas comes in a few days, I will still miss my family as I always do. I will long for the day when I can finally be with my fiancée during this precious time of year. She and I will acknowledge and celebrate in a small way that we are yet another year closer to having that long-awaited precious time together. I will enjoy a special turkey dinner here in prison for the eleventh time and look forward to calling distant relatives to wish them a merry Christmas.

I will also — and most importantly — take a moment of solitude during the day to pray, reflect, and acknowledge the most Powerful Force in my life and what He has done to dramatically change my world for the better. I will thank Him for loving me when I needed it the most and for guiding me when I was surely lost with no map to where I was headed. I will thank Him for giving me the strength to make it through this situation day after day, week after week, month after month, and year after year. I will tell Him how much I appreciate the amazing woman He has blessed me with when I deserved her the least. I will reiterate to Him that I am eternally grateful for His belief in me and for providing me with the gift of understanding and relating to people in an impactful way. In essence, I will thank Him for His divine intervention in my life.

A REASON TO BE SELFISH

The new year brings countless goals that are set by reinvigorated people who are, in this moment, determined more than ever to change an aspect of their lives that they feel has held them back in some way. We commonly refer to these lofty goals as New Year's resolutions. I'm not certain what the statistics are of those who stick to these goals long term, but if I had to guess, I'd imagine it is less than fifty percent. Why is this? People identify very clear goals every year (i.e., to lose weight, quit smoking or give up some other harmful habit), yet often only a few short months later their daily habits no longer reflect their impassioned desire to change. They have seemingly given up and resigned themselves to continue whatever it is they would ultimately like to overcome.

I can readily recall too many failed attempts in my own life of achieving goals, but in retrospect I have also noticed these were goals I aspired to meet for the sake of appeasing others. I wanted to be financially successful so people would think highly of me. I tried to curb my excessive drinking to get my then-girlfriend to stop nagging me about it. These were "goals" that never materialized because I've come to understand the only way I can develop and sustain the necessary level of commitment and motivation to reach these goals is to do it for *myself* — not someone else.

It is encouraging to hear many men in prison say they want to get out of prison, land a respectable job, abstain from drugs and alcohol, and become family men for the sake of their kids and wives. On the surface, most would say these are aspirations anyone in society would support for men who are newly released from prison, and I don't disagree. I do, however, question the viability and likelihood of these goals coming to fruition under this pretense. Allow me to explain.

Although these are great goals to have and are not inherently wrong or misguided, they are not derived from the necessary source of motivation to be successfully carried out. These motivations (primarily family-based), as we've seen over and over, can only fuel a person's efforts so much. In the end, it is the individual's personal reinforcement mechanisms (internal rewards and satisfaction) that will win out. If someone is not fully committed to achieving their goals for their own personal reasons, they will inevitably lose their fervor and drive to continue striving for goals they feel are more of a burden or obligation than a personal reward.

When I came to prison (this time), I understood the importance and urgency of making drastic changes from within that required confronting deep-seated issues that had plagued me since adolescence. I undertook this endeavor not for my family but for myself. As much as I love them, I had to do this for myself if I was going to do it seriously and diligently. I knew if I was going to leave prison a better, more educated, mature man with a greater quality of life, it would be imperative that I change for me — no one else. The by-product of this effort is that my family will still obviously benefit from my growth. But the fact remains that ultimately the one who drives me is me!

From year to year I have set defined, specific goals that I persistently strive toward and know will make me a more productive person. I have addressed my selfishness, impatience (although my fiancée will be quick to remind me that I'm still a work in progress), and excessive need to gain others' approval for validation and self-worth. Although I have not completely conquered these deficiencies, I'm pleased to know I am much better today than I was over eleven years ago. Despite my triumphs in these areas of my life, my efforts remain as strong today as they were when I initially started this endeavor because they are innately important to me, not because I'm attempting to gain someone else's approval or acceptance.

Going into this new year, therefore, I encourage all of you who are setting goals (not ritualistic resolutions for the sake of keeping tradition) to do them for *yourself* — no one else! Others will benefit from your progress, but they should not be the primary motivation for your efforts. Set clear, defined goals that can be measured by tangible results. Allow yourself room to fall short, but don't settle for failure. Encourage your incarcerated loved one to tackle at least one area of their life that will improve their character this year. Reiterate to them, however, that their efforts cannot be for someone else; it has to be for themselves. This happens to be one of the very few reasons that it's not only okay for someone to be selfish — it's imperative! Good luck in the new year.

RETRIBUTION OR REHABILITATION?

What is the best, most effective approach to dealing with prisoners? Should the criminal justice system primarily be used to punish those who violate the law and are sentenced to prison? Or should it rather serve as a mechanism for rehabilitation? This dichotomous question is a polarizing one that aligns people on opposite sides of this argument and has shaped our penal system since its inception.

When men and women come to prison, we invariably cost hard-working, law-abiding taxpayers across this country billions of dollars annually to feed, clothe, and house us. Our water, heat, medical and dental care are all paid for in full on the backs of hard-working Americans from all walks of life. Recidivism rates show that most us who are eventually released will re-offend and return to these overcrowded prisons within five years, causing taxpayers yet many more billions of dollars for our lengthy terms of incarceration. This perpetual, bleak trend will, unfortunately, remain intact if prisons continue to be used to primarily warehouse inmates.

Statistics show the higher the education one attains while incarcerated, the greater the likelihood of his or her success in the community, and the lesser likelihood he/she will return to prison. Subsequently, the longer he or she thrives in a productive role in society, the more he/she is able to pay back society through tax dollars generated from their own productivity, which is largely made possible by earning a college degree or becoming certified in a trade while in prison.

Having noted these impressive outcomes, I know it is also paramount that the individual who breaks the law pays for his/her crime by serving time in prison. But the sensible thing to do to ensure that prison doesn't continue to have a revolving door that perpetually costs taxpayers and state budgets billions of dollars over time is to educate prisoners so they can begin to contribute to society. Offer apprenticeship programs so they can become electricians, plumbers, and construction workers when they are released from prison. When people have more at stake to lose, they tend to think twice about risking it by doing something illegal.

Many would vociferously rebut this stance by saying, "So, we're just supposed to reward law breakers with a free college education?" My answer would be, "No. You don't have to offer any education of value at all, but either way you're going to spend those same tax dollars — either on lengthy incarcerations or on education that would enable newly-released inmates to pay back society in an economically meaningful way. Which scenario is better for society in the long run?"

I am dismayed and appalled that this remarkable country that offers abundant opportunity on one hand can simultaneously incarcerate more people per capita than any other nation on earth! We've become a nation that would rather warehouse human lives in the name of retribution than rehabilitate people for the greater good of our collective society. Ironically, every state in the union includes the word "corrections" in reference to its prison system. The (fill-in-the-state) Department of Corrections sounds like it is a department that is primarily — if not solely — designed for correcting or rehabilitating its occupants. Hmmm . . . this is paradoxical to say the least.

Personally, I'm extremely blessed to have had the financial means and support of loved ones that have enabled me to attain college degrees. This undoubtedly gives me a great advantage over thousands of other incarcerated men and women in my state. But it disheartens me when I think of the lack of opportunity for countless others because for many years of their lives (albeit often by their own fault) they have been institutionalized with no real opportunity to rehabilitate themselves and gain something tangible to show for it. Sadly, to say, this unspeakable trend will continue if retribution over rehabilitation continues to be our country's motive for incarceration.

INCARCERATED MENTALITY

As a Black man, I take immense pride in knowing what my ancestors overcame hundreds of years ago amid the heinous, inhuman conditions they were forced to endure. It empowers me to know I come from a lineage of people who could muster the mental and physical mettle to persevere through such horrific circumstances and not succumb to them. I have found myself invoking their relentless spirit of determination of not allowing my physical circumstances to suppress my drive to be better, achieve more, and experience a greater life than I have ever known.

Their unparalleled resolve to have basic freedoms in life came in the form of sneaking out late at night to clandestine locations to congregate and teach each other to read, conduct church, and marry. In the face of risking death, they were not deterred in pursuing what they desperately longed for and refused to live without. The human spirit and tenacity are such powerful forces! One of the things I have personally learned from the atrocities of slavery in this country is to not allow my physical circumstance to limit my imagination, thoughts, and ability to mentally rise above the limitations of my situation. Said differently, incarceration can be more than a physical prison — it can also become a state of mind.

Many men and women in prison have lived lives that have been plagued by emotional turmoil, poor self-esteem, and profound rejection. Poor upbringings mired in physical/mental abuse are just the beginning of some of their jarring life stories. In no way do I highlight these points to attempt to offer an excuse for unlawful behavior. We did the crime and now we are obligated to do the time — period. However, I assert these facts to offer a possible *explanation* for the causes of much of the deviant behavior that has brought many of us to prison. And, more importantly, I highlight these things to say these character defects often continue to dictate the lives of inmates across the nation.

Many who are incarcerated have wholeheartedly believed throughout their lives that they would never succeed, so why even try? They have internalized the notion that they are worthless because, after all, their parents (and others) told them this all their lives, and society reinforces it after they're released. When several people tell you that you smell, you subconsciously feel insecure and begin to sniff yourself throughout the day to see if their accusation is true. We base much of our view of ourselves on people's opinions of us and how they react to us — but we shouldn't!

This is a defeatist mentality that inevitably stunts our mental growth and cripples our ability to fulfill our destiny and purpose in life. We fall victim to allowing those who despise us for no good reason to prevent us from reaching our fullest potential and having the lives we were meant to lead.

Life is far too short and precious to allow people or circumstances to determine how we spend it. We have an inherent ability to transcend, so no one or no physical barrier should be oppressive enough to cause us to ever adopt an incarcerated mentality.

OBSTACLES = OPPORTUNITIES

Life is tough — there are no two ways about it. Unforeseen tragedies occur and sudden crises emerge that turn our lives upside-down in an instant. Unrelenting misfortune can plague a person or family for years to come with seemingly no rational antecedent to explain its occurrence. But what should we do when disaster strikes? What options do we have when very difficult obstacles are abruptly placed before us?

As humans, we have developed brains that are complex and sophisticated enough to adapt to virtually any given situation, whether we've been exposed to that circumstance previously or not. Many animals, however, are not equipped with these mechanisms. They must strictly rely on their natural instincts for survival and adaptation — but not us. Unlike animals, we are able to quickly conjure solutions to new problems by recalling information/behaviors we've previously learned, having experienced similar situations, or seeing someone else go through them. Because of these innate skills, we can thrive in strenuous, mentally-taxing situations of many kinds. The question then becomes, do we succumb to these novel stressors, or do we choose to use our God-given resources to thrive in adverse circumstances?

When I — and many others, I imagine — came to prison, I made a conscious decision to not view this as an insurmountable obstacle that couldn't be used for something positive. Instead, I *chose* to perceive it as an opportunity. An opportunity for what, you ask? Glad you asked. This became a prime opportunity for me to thoroughly and honestly search within myself without distraction or interference from people or sources that I surrounded myself with before I came here. It was my opportunity to finally discover what I felt would bring me the most satisfaction in life (professionally and personally). Prison became my laboratory of sorts to be creative and "experiment" with various endeavors to determine exactly which one would fulfill me internally and lead me to a purpose-filled life.

Like prison, life in general presents many challenging obstacles that can be converted into opportunities to facilitate inner-growth and newfound perspectives that are not spurred by typical, mundane circumstances. The loss of a job, divorce, and even the death of a close loved one are all examples of tremendous, life-changing hardships that can be used to induce intense reflection and growth — if we choose to!

Many of you know that I'm a huge proponent of the "mind over matter" mentality. In other words, I strongly believe we all have the capacity and ability to choose to approach *any* situation from a positive, constructive viewpoint. We have the choice of pouting and doing nothing about it when life throws us a curve ball of affliction, or we can choose to accept it, work on bringing a positive outcome to it, and resolve to become better because of it. This crisis can, for instance, come in the form of a life-without-parole sentence, but if we make the firm decision to view it as a unique opportunity to self-reflect, learn and grow spiritually and mentally, then the circumstance loses its power over us that it was intended to have; it cannot defeat the individual who determines not to allow it to. Instead, it can serve as a profound opportunity for learning and self-discovery.

The next time you are in what seems to be an insurmountable set of circumstances, I encourage you to *choose* to look at it from a different perspective. Ask yourself, "What can I personally gain from this? How can I use this to better myself?" But remember, the answer may not come right away, so be patient. In short, teach yourself to begin to view your obstacles as opportunities.

CAMOUFLAGED BLESSINGS

When we think of blessings in a traditional sense, we typically think of things that are inherently good or wholesome: finding a much-needed job, giving birth to a healthy baby, or finding your soul mate. These, and countless other events and occurrences of good fortune, are all viewed as things we should be, and often are, grateful for. Although these things of obvious value ought to be appreciated and acknowledged as such, what about the things that occur in life that seem to have no apparent value? Even more so, what about things that are traumatic, stressful, and downright burdensome? What do we make of those events?

I highly doubt that any of us who stood before a judge who was wearing an all-important black robe while sitting behind a regal, intimidating desk as they rendered their punishment for the next however many years thought this was a moment of good fortune, or a blessing. However, I cannot tell you how many people I've met while in prison who have admitted their incarceration turned out to be their "blessing in disguise" or their "camouflaged blessing."

Personally, I thought my life was over when the judge sentenced me to two hundred and ten months — day for day! I could not see the light at the end of the tunnel. Forget the light, I couldn't even see the opening of the tunnel I was about to enter! But it didn't take long for me to realize that what I had before me was a unique opportunity to learn, grow, and establish a clear direction in my life. I discovered my inner passions that I knew would bring me genuine happiness and fulfillment if I made it my life's mission to vigorously pursue them. The opportunity to recover from alcohol and learn how to confront and work through emotional pain and turmoil without substances has been invaluable. This situation has enabled me to cultivate a solid, healthy identity while giving me a sense of purpose and self-worth I never had — or knew I could have — prior to this experience.

Traumatic, arduous circumstances tend to have profound, unique ways of revealing our innate mettle and fortitude that many of us never knew we possessed. They tend to break us down and rebuild us into better, wiser, more resilient versions of ourselves. They force us to take an honest — often painful — inventory of our lives and assess where we've been, where we are, and where we want to go as we understand how our actions have led us to where we are and can lead us to new places in the future if we make the necessary changes. We essentially begin to look at life through a clearer, more perceptive lens that brings into focus all the things that truly matter. We intuitively know what we need to do to realize our goals and lead us where we want to end up.

No one gladly welcomes life's most difficult circumstances. Given a choice, rational thought and human nature would dictate that no one would opt to go through periods of hardship, crisis, or uncertainty. But what a disservice we would do to ourselves if we shunned the very circumstances that are able to help us grow immensely and become the people we ultimately want to be, doing the things we envision ourselves doing. We would be depriving ourselves of extraordinary opportunities to discover profound truths about ourselves that, I believe, other situations cannot yield. As a result, we would settle for a life of mediocrity and unfulfillment. Sadly, we would rob ourselves of the rare opportunity to grow and discover who we really are through our camouflaged blessings.

A PURPOSE FOR EVERYTHING

When I sat in the county jail over ten years ago awaiting sentencing and not knowing my fate (but knowing I was facing anywhere between ten and twenty years), I could not see any silver lining or find solace in my circumstance. I was depressed and tried my best to fervently pray to God for leniency, yet not truly believing it would be granted. Like most people who are faced with a tremendously difficult situation and loss of control over it, I attempted to bargain my way out of it: "God, if you just get me out of this one, I promise I'll quit drinking and I'll go to church and praise you every Sunday." My wishes were not granted in the way I'd hoped.

Eleven years later, I now see exactly why I was not allowed to simply walk out of jail or receive a lenient sentence. I've come to fully understand that it was purposeful that I spend the next seventeen and a half years in prison. There are two primary reasons why it was essential and to my benefit that I got sentenced to this amount of time: to prepare me to carry out my God-given purpose and to be of comfort to others along the way. For now, I'd like to focus on the latter.

As many of you know, my goal is to counsel young men and women who struggle with substance addiction and/or behavioral issues. I have invested a lot of money and years into pursuing my education to bring this goal to fruition. But I've also come to understand that this is only half of what makes a successful counselor. The other half would be life experience.

As I have now had many years to acquire immeasurable insight about myself, past behaviors, and faulty thinking patterns, I can confidently say that I've gone through *all* that I have so I can help others.

Sure, in the moments where I made poor decisions and exhibited self-destructive behavior that would have grave consequences, I could not see any value in it. Today, however, I see clearly why I went through the many obstacles that I have. It is this revelation that has also confirmed that I am best utilized when I counsel others who are going through similar trials. I know with certainty that hardships, adversities, and the perseverance that has enabled me to overcome life's challenges occurred because it was necessary that I live through these things in order to inspire and help others in their time of need. You cannot help others if you haven't gone through what they are going through. You cannot offer them what you yourself have never had.

Knowing this then, I no longer question why certain things have happened in my life. I know that I am — just as others are — supposed to use my experiences to provide solace, comfort, and wisdom to others. Unfortunately, many of us in prison do not realize this truth and continue to live in a way that does nothing to help ourselves, let alone those who could greatly benefit from our insight and knowledge. Those important opportunities that ought to serve as invaluable life lessons are, tragically, spent in vain.

I'm utterly amazed at how life's most difficult experiences can be absorbed and later used to aid others. It is a true testament to the ability and tenacity of the human spirit to confront challenging circumstances head on and turn them into positive outcomes that have a lifelong benefit for ourselves and others. This lends to the profound notion that nothing — *nothing* — happens without reason. Said differently, there is a purpose for everything.

JAILHOUSE RELIGION

Is it coincidence that many people who are incarcerated seem to suddenly "get religion" or "find God"? Or is it a truly genuine admission in the face of hopelessness of one's failed ways of living and an adoption of a Higher Power to guide their lives? I presume many people (both incarcerated and not) are immediately skeptical when inmates suddenly begin carrying a bible everywhere they go and speaking zealously with anyone who will listen about how miraculously God has changed their lives and given them renewed hope. Others scoff and utter such things as, "They sure weren't following God when they were out" or "Where was all this piety when they were victimizing people?" These are fair points, but I don't believe the conversation should end there.

It turns out that I happen to be one of those people who "found God" when I came to prison. I don't, however, wear my faith on my sleeve, but the principles I apply to my life are directly rooted in my belief in God and aid me on this tumultuous journey daily. People will often turn to an "outside source" for comfort, understanding, and strength when they find themselves in an extremely stressful, hopeless, seemingly insurmountable situation. This is understandable since psychological trauma can only be mitigated by psychological comfort. If people believe there is a Being that is larger, more powerful, and able to control situations that they themselves can't, they will relinquish their control over trying to make sense of their plight and begin to view it through the lens of a Higher Power ultimately being in control.

I do not make these points as an attempt to legitimize or discredit the perceived validity of people's genuineness in what they believe — that's not my point. What I *am* trying to say is whether it be religion, yoga, or anything else that provides some psychological relief that people need as they go through tremendously difficult circumstances, we *all* turn to something or someone. I find it ironic that people would ridicule and question inmates' seriousness and genuineness when they are merely trying to search for a constructive way to mentally overcome their arduous situation. And who knows, maybe their newfound beliefs and adherence to the religious principles they've adopted while incarcerated will turn out to be the pivotal point that will change their lives forever. Who is anyone to judge or criticize them (and me) for that? Would you rather the alternative: inmates engaging in gang activity, extortion, violence, and wasting this critical time in their lives?

I personally think the friends and family members of those incarcerated (as well as society at large) would much rather see their loved ones subscribe to a religion and its principles than engage in using drugs or drinking "pruno" (homemade jailhouse alcohol) to cope with their situation. And if they then abandon their religion after they are released, are they automatically worse off for having picked it up in the first place? I operate from the belief that all humans seek some form of comfort in their worst of times to cope with the psychological anguish; and if religion is what gets people through this profoundly difficult time, then who can legitimately criticize them for that, especially when they themselves haven't gone through such a circumstance?

GOD, GRANT ME THE SERENITY

In Alcoholics Anonymous there is a well-known prayer that is used by all its members to help with the arduous nature of leading a life of recovery. It goes like this: God, grant me the serenity to accept the things I cannot change, the courage to change the things I can, and the wisdom to know the difference. Admittedly, I do not attend AA meetings on a regular basis (though I have in the past), but this simple prayer has resonated with me ever since I heard it for the first time because of its profound — yet simple — message that I can apply to my life on a daily basis.

The first part of this message says, "God, grant me the serenity to accept the things I cannot change." This plea speaks to the desire one has to be able to accept — or come to peace with — the hardships in life that we have no control over. When I first came to prison, I went through a period of intense self-pity and helplessness that was due to the deprivation I felt from being cut off from life's simple freedoms and the loss of control over my own fate. There came a point during this transitional phase from freedom to captivity that demanded I accept the reality that I couldn't control the outcome (in terms of how much time I'd end up serving in prison). However, I came to understand that although I couldn't change what happened to me, I *could* change how I responded to it. I had the choice of whether I would choose to use this time for good or not; it didn't take long for me to grasp the fact that the sooner I accepted this simple truth, the sooner I could alleviate an enormous amount of stress and begin the process of change and productivity. This brings me to the next concept within this prayer.

The next part says, "... the courage to change the things I can." This part of the AA prayer is what I invoked when I decided I would do the very best I could to convert this horrible tragedy into an uplifting, empowering, self-enhancing experience. True enough, I'd accepted the fact I was going to be incarcerated for over seventeen years no matter what. But the critical question then became, what was I going to do with it? How was I going to best utilize this time? I resolved I would concentrate my efforts on mentoring the men that I encountered while here. I would dignify my life and those affected by my actions by devoting myself to being of service to others. I determined I would be released from prison a much better man. I had accepted the fact I couldn't change my physical circumstance, but I *could* change how I approached my imprisonment and what I made of it. This now brings me to the conclusion of this prayer.

The last component says, ". . .and the wisdom to know the difference." It has been imperative for me to be able to discern the difference between things I can control and those I can't. I make every attempt to put my energy and effort into things I have a level of control over (i.e. how I use my time, how I conduct myself) while not concerning myself with or dwelling on those I don't. It's certainly not always easy to carry out this principle because, as many of you can attest, we generally want to exert our control over many situations that concern us and cause us stress, but we also know we'd be much better off not wasting energy and emotion over these things that we cannot control. By placing my energy into things that I can control, I have been able to maximize my efforts, reduce my stress level, and stay motivated to meet my goals.

The principles of this remarkable prayer have unequivocally been the driving force behind the way I handle myself and the successes I've had throughout this extremely difficult time. And just as it has become a monumental centerpiece in *my* life and has aided me in fulfilling my purpose, I know it can serve you in the same way. No amount or type of adversity is insurmountable! It merely boils down to how you *choose* to approach it and what you determine to make of it. My personal recommendation is you approach it with these simple words: "God, grant me the serenity."

IF I CAN DO IT . . .

From time to time I find myself in deep contemplation over what I've accomplished during these eleven years of incarceration. This is, however, a somewhat rare occurrence for me because I'm constantly looking ahead to the next goal that I seek to accomplish. It's very important that I stay committed to achieving my goals because after seventeen years in prison, I had better have a lot to show for it! And when I do take a moment to breathe and actually consider that I've earned two degrees from major universities, a certificate from another prominent university, published my memoir, and am currently more than halfway through the completion of a master's degree, it both humbles and fills me with gratitude for having had the rare opportunity to do these things while in this situation. My story is not what it is merely because of what I've been able to accomplish, however; it is significant more so because of where I come from — in more ways than one.

For those who have read my memoir *Palpable Irony*, you know I did not graduate from high school. I lacked confidence in many areas of my adolescent life and, therefore, turned to alcohol to numb the pain of feeling inadequate. No one in my immediate family had ever gone beyond high school, and there was certainly no reason for me to believe I would break that trend. When I embarked on this incredibly long journey over ten years ago, however, that all changed.

Academics were never my strength, so when I came to prison, I was not particularly confident in my ability to succeed in a classroom setting. Having said that, I was determined to still give it my best effort because I'd made up my mind that I needed to take my life in a new direction. With the first college class I took (Humanities), I gained a little confidence because I fared well with some help from the instructor. This was enough to compel me to continue this academic path. Wait, allow me to slightly backtrack; it was the completion of my GED several years earlier that provided the initial spark of confidence that in turn gave me the courage to sign up for a college course in the first place. After my first small victory at the collegiate level, though, I *knew* I could do it — and I have!

I did manage to surprise myself with each class I took, though, because despite the level of difficulty, I still consistently got A's and B's. I kept my focus on the work until I eventually acquired my AA, then it was my BS, then the certificate, then the book, and now the master's. By staying dialed in on one goal at a time and not getting ahead of myself — which would have caused me to become overwhelmed — I've been able to reach each successive goal, and here I am years later having accomplished things I never would have thought possible.

I have used my educational journey to mentor and work with young men in prison through tutoring in the education department. I encourage them through their educational endeavors, reminding them that I too sat in that very seat and earned my GED years ago. It's important that I show them I was (and am) just like them because, like me, if they apply themselves, they can also achieve their goals. I let them know I have applied myself and in doing so have overcome extremely low self-esteem, shyness, and alcoholism. I grew up in "the 'hood," ran with gangs, carried guns, sold crack cocaine, and got involved in a lot more mischief and criminal activity during my adolescent years than most people who know me today would believe. Yet, here I am a published author, holding college degrees, eager to use my experience to help others.

My point for highlighting these things is not to heap praise on myself — not in the least. It is solely to show that if I of all people can come from having a severely broken spirit, growing up in an extremely adverse environment, and going through the tremendous hardships that I have while still accomplishing my goals through arduous work and devotion, then I believe *anyone* can do the same. I illustrate my hurdles and milestones to be an inspiration to others in prison who, undoubtedly, come from similar backgrounds and circumstances. Let my story be a testament to all who struggle with self-esteem and lack confidence in their ability to succeed that they too can achieve things they never thought possible. Believe me when I say that if I can do it, *you* can do it too!

DOWN PAYMENT

When I was sentenced, it was said that my lengthy sentence was my "payment" for the "debt" that I owed society through my victimization of those I'd "offended." This is the analogy that we often hear referenced across the board when someone is sentenced. It's as if every day that I'm incarcerated, it's symbolic of me writing a check payable to "Mr." or "Mrs. Society" and mailing it off to an account that benefits society at large.

I illustrate it this way not to be flippant but to highlight the inadequacy of this analogy. Think about this: when we come to prison for the horrendous things we've done, how many lives have been affected? Many, right? Aside from the victims themselves, countless children have been (and continue to be) affected by Dad not being there to help raise them; parents and siblings, wives and girlfriends, and many others are irreparably impacted by our costly actions. These references don't even consider the significant economic impact of wages lost due to the psychological effects of having been victimized by crime, rendering them unable to work or do so effectively. Therefore, when considered from this perspective, how can the analogy be made, in fairness, that by merely completing our sentence we've repaired our damage to society? That we've paid our debt to society, so to speak?

I am of the mindset that for me to *fully* repay society for the incalculable damage I've wreaked on countless lives, I must spend the rest of my life striving to make a meaningful difference in the lives of others. This is the *true* repayment, if you will, that I can offer society for atonement of my offenses against it. Using this experience to gain insight that I can then pass along to the next generation is a payment that society will benefit from in a tangible way — not me merely serving over seventeen years in prison and being released to carry out the rest of my life as I please. How would that benefit society?

Being in prison does not necessarily benefit society — not in a sense that is truly felt. Sure, people who break the law *need* to be punished, and prison is certainly the necessary penalty for many crimes committed. I need to be in prison for what I did — that's not my argument. But let's not misconstrue punishment alone as a direct benefit to society. It would be shortsighted and misguided to believe that I'm paying what I owe society by simply being isolated from it for seventeen years. This part of my debt should merely be the beginning of my repayment to society.

Put another way, picture this scenario: A father is walking with his two young children and wife along a dirt trail in the mountains. He travels ahead of them a few paces and slips into a small ditch that was concealed by brush. What would this man's logical response be to this occurrence? The natural thing to do would be to first gather himself, turn back to his family, and warn them of the pitfall ahead. This is tantamount to what I believe my duty is to the younger generation. This is me giving back to society what it rightfully deserves for my abuse of it.

Many may disagree with the notion that we will only truly pay off our debt to society if we devote ourselves to a life of service to the younger generation after we've completed our sentence. After all, they'll say, the law and the judge's sentence only mandated we serve a term of imprisonment — not a life of helping others thereafter. And, factually, they would not be wrong, but my point obviously goes beyond surface facts. It would be a fruitless waste of time (as we often see) if a lengthy term of incarceration were not followed up with a duty to warn and work with those following behind you in your community and society. This would be equivalent to the father on the trail simply pulling himself out of the ditch and continuing on the path, not warning his family of the perils that await them if they don't deviate from their current course. Viewed in this light, my incarceration alone is, therefore, not sufficient payment to society for the destruction I've caused — it is merely a down payment.

MAKING PAYMENTS

My last blog ("Down Payment") was written to make the point through analogy that merely serving time in prison is not sufficient payment to society after victimizing people and causing great harm to our communities. My point was that to actually and meaningfully begin to repay society for one's harms, one must make a sustained effort to help guide and warn the younger generations of what things to avoid and what paths to steer clear of.

During a period of incarceration, I believe it is an inmate's responsibility to begin to work on the character flaws that ultimately led him/her to prison. It is his/her responsibility to try to gain an understanding of faulty thinking patterns that have been used to perpetuate irrational thinking and subsequent behavior that runs contrary to societal rules and values, eventually causing them to violate the law and end up in prison.

In my own case, when I began to work on and conduct myself in a way that was respectable and I could be proud of, it gave me credibility with those whom I aspired to reach through mentoring. I have had the opportunity to mentor, educate, and befriend many young (and older) men over the years who have both taught me and been taught by me about many important aspects of life. I personally view this as a way society will likely benefit from my incarceration because when some of these young men are released, they'll now take a new, positive approach to life. Maybe they will use this newfound perspective to motivate them to abide by societal rules, get a job, and become better fathers to their children. Are these lofty goals? Sure, but everyone should have a dream and a vision before they can become a reality. And it's nothing special that I do to plant this seed of hope; I merely take the time to listen to their thoughts, concerns, and interests, which has proven to be profoundly impactful in getting these men to open up and be receptive to new ideas and possibilities. Many young people in today's world, I've discovered, tend to misbehave in numerous ways simply as a means be heard, to be paid attention to. Taking time out of my day to lend a sympathetic ear to these men has been therapeutic for the both of us.

Aside from using my time to be a positive role model to other inmates, I believe another way to start making "payments" toward the huge debt that we owe society is to begin to mend relationships with family members (and others) that we've hurt through manipulation and other selfishly-driven motives. Of course, we all know the proof of genuine contrition will be revealed in our actions that follow our release from incarceration, but I do subscribe to the notion that there is no better time to show I'm sorry than now. Working to rebuild these invaluable bonds with people we've wronged is critical because there is a likelihood that this network of people will also be our voice of reason and primary support system when we get out. Even if things don't work out ideally, it still can be beneficial from the standpoint of displaying humility and accountability for one's harmful actions to other people. This is a testament to the transformation process taking root and bearing fruit.

I have done my very best to address my issues and work at becoming the best Martin I can be because I know this is required for me to effectively reach and teach others in a way that will have a lasting impact on their lives. If I'm successful in this effort, then I'm confident my community will be the beneficiary of my actions in some way or another — even if I never see it for myself. If my community benefits from my efforts, then it logically follows that those I have helped will directly (or indirectly) positively affect their communities as well — one life at a time. In my estimation, making down payments toward the debt we owe society is best done by being of service to others.

MY THERAPY

Prior to a few months ago, the thought of becoming a blogger had never crossed my mind. I had no clue what people typically blogged about, who read them, how often, how to get started or anything else related to the endeavor. Then I received a letter from a woman who had read my memoir, enjoyed it, and soon became a pen pal. Shortly into our correspondence she inquired what my long-term goals were regarding writing while in prison, my career aspirations *after* prison, and anything else I envisioned doing with my life. When I expressed to her that I sought to help as many people as possible through counseling, speaking, and writing, she immediately sensed my passion and commitment to helping people and offered her assistance in this vision. She then informed me that I didn't have to wait until I was released to do this — there was a way I could start doing it from prison!

She suggested I begin to write blogs that would shine a light on issues that people who have incarcerated loved ones are affected by. With my first-hand experience, I felt confident in my ability to write compelling, insightful blogs that my target audience (and perhaps even a few detractors) would appreciate and benefit from. After deciding to undertake this mission, I sat down and began writing my first blog.

Here we are only two months into this effort, and I must say it has already far exceeded what I thought and expected it would be. I am pleasantly surprised and humbled by the tremendous amount of support and validation I've received from many of you who read my blogs weekly. It truly inspires me to write when I know there are many people who identify with what I'm saying and find meaning and insight in what I offer. It touches my soul when some of you take the time to comment, share your personal stories that relate to my blogs, and assure me that what I write resonates with you in a profound way.

A friend of mine (a fellow inmate) surprised me when he told me his loved one had read *all* of my blogs and said they serve as a form of "therapy" for her. I don't know if I'm worthy of such high praise, but I was incredibly touched and deeply humbled by that validation. To be in my position — where I'm completely detached from the physical world beyond these walls — yet have a burning desire to give back to society in a meaningful way, is extremely difficult. But when I am given the opportunity to share my individual experiences, thoughts, and opinions that seem to provide many of you with useful information that helps you and your incarcerated loved ones, it gives me an extraordinary sense of satisfaction, purpose, and reward. I am fulfilled when I know I am making a positive impact on someone's life. For that, I thank all of you who take the time to read and comment on my blogs; it truly means the world to me. You've given me the inspiration and confidence to continue writing for years to come.

It's ironic that I went into this (writing blogs) with the intention of offering help and support to those of you with incarcerated loved ones, not realizing that it would be reciprocated. Thank you all for supporting my efforts. Thank you for being *my* therapy.

LET'S BE HONEST

Let me begin by saying I am extremely grateful for the opportunity to express my views and share my insights with those of you who regularly read and are encouraged by what I write. I am also appreciative for all of you who have read my blogs and responded with great, honest feedback of what you have gained from my words, as well as sharing how you are supporting your incarcerated loved ones to the best of your ability. Having said this, however, I'd like to address a scathing opinion held by those who believe, by and large, that prisoners attend religious services merely as a guise to manipulate and take advantage of young, unsuspecting inmates.

I recently wrote a blog about the benefit religion can have for inmates who seek a Power greater than themselves to ease the pain and anguish of this grueling situation. However, I'm now aware there are some who believe religious services in prison are nothing but a cover for predators who wish to identify and gain influence over new, young inmates who are seeking guidance from more experienced religious inmates. Indeed, predators of all kinds will look for creative, discreet ways to manipulate their potential victims, but in no way do the actions of a few (and it is a scant minority) justify the accusation that this represents the motives of *most* inmates who attend these services. In my experience, I have not seen or heard of this happening. However, while my personal experience is not evidence that it doesn't happen, the same goes for the people who make the accusation that this is the underlying motive that leads inmates to join religious services.

If we applied this same notion to churches in our society where we have seen numerous priests be accused of molestation of young boys, we'd condemn the entire religious leadership. But would this be fair? Would this be a justified indictment? Would this even be an accurate assessment? As repulsed as we are with the heinous actions committed by some — a few, in fact — we must temper our emotions with the reality that those accused of these horrific crimes are but a miniscule portion of the clergy in that religious group. Our rational mind then tells us we cannot and ought not paint the entire church and its members with a broad brush of condemnation.

I don't fault individuals for expressing their impassioned disdain for despicable acts committed against young, vulnerable victims who come to a place of worship seeking guidance. Whether in here or out there, we all ought to be outraged when this happens. However, holding everyone accountable for the actions of a few is just as egregious and deplorable. It is always a dangerous and slippery slope to stereotype a group of people based on the actions of a few as this inevitably perpetuates discrimination and prejudice. We can be outspoken about things that offend us — and we should be; but it is equally important to maintain a rational mind because this enables us to speak assertively about our grievances while having fruitful dialogue with those who see it differently. Honest conversations about sensitive topics are necessary in a society as diverse as ours. But the key word here is *honest* — not slanted, biased, or misleading. To make the offensive assertion that all inmates attend religious services for the sole purpose of deceiving and taking advantage of impressionable younger inmates is offensive and dishonest.

INMATES GIVING BACK

I was pleasantly astonished to arrive here over a month ago and discover I could purchase an assortment of meals that consist of Papa Murphy's pizza, Chinese food, barbeque cheese burgers, sausage, hot dogs, hot links, Doritos, blueberry pancakes, Captain Crunch cereal, steak, and too much more to list here! Throughout my entire ten years spent at a different prison, I had never had this luxury.

I gleefully called to share with my family and loved ones how excited I was to have the opportunity to taste these delicious foods that I hadn't tasted in ten years. I realized most inmates would never have access to these things, so I most certainly appreciated my good fortune. My family, of course, was very happy that I would be able to have these things to look forward to; nevertheless, they implored me to stay cognizant of my health and limit my indulgence in these not-so-healthy treats.

It wasn't until one week later (after the initial excitement and novelty subsided) that I learned why these meals were routinely made available for us to purchase. Then I became *really* impressed!

I learned that many of these food items were fundraisers for various charitable causes. I discovered one of these charities was Camp Agape, a summer camp for children who have at least one incarcerated parent. During this weeklong camp, kids enjoy positive recreation, education, support, and reprieve from their otherwise challenging environments. This annual fundraiser generates a lot of money in donations for this worthy cause.

Another recent fundraiser offered large muffins for purchase. I was informed the proceeds for this would go toward purchasing more yarn, needles, and crochet materials. Yes, I said *crochet!* Inmates hand-crochet beautiful blankets and other items that are then either sold or donated to foundations that need blankets for homeless individuals. The proceeds then go to an organization that supports children who are cancer-stricken. *Wow*, I thought. Suddenly I became more thrilled and intrigued to know I was contributing to more noble causes than merely filling my belly with food I didn't normally get to eat. I was encouraged to know my purchases were being used to provide a small amount of comfort to someone down on their luck and in need of a warm blanket, or a kid who could enjoy a week of fun.

I do not write these things to garner praise for these efforts, nor do I mention them in an attempt to paint a rosy picture that attempts to mitigate the severe damage inmates have caused society — I know better than that. My sole purpose is to highlight the fact that, despite what most people believe about prisons, inmates, and the motives of those incarcerated, it's rather refreshing to see a contradiction of these stereotypes. It's gratifying to know I can finally be a part of the solution — not just the problem.

A STORY THAT NEEDED TO BE TOLD

Approximately four years ago my girlfriend urged me, "Babe, you should write a book about your life story; I think it would inspire people." Initially, I paid no serious attention to her suggestion because I thought there was no way I would even know how to compose such a book, and secondly, I figured no one (aside from family and friends, of course) would be interested in reading it. In other words, I had no real interest in undertaking such a task.

Months later she prompted me again, and this time I listened more earnestly because I began to feel, in fact, I had a lot to share in terms of how I've used my ability to overcome adversities and inspire others who are going through extremely difficult circumstances. After some thought, I determined I would use my story to show people from all walks of life that no matter how insurmountable situations may appear, you *can* overcome them, use them to your advantage, and emerge more resilient and wiser for having gone through them.

I decided I'd write the book. It took nearly seven months to complete. It was important for me to write it in a way that was relatable, conversational, honest, and compelling in order to reach as many people as I could — particularly people in the midst of their own storm. We often find it virtually impossible to see the potential value or meaning in a lengthy term of incarceration, but my book makes it crystal clear how this *can* happen and why it is essential that it *does* happen.

Palpable Irony was a story that needed to be told because we all go through harrowing situations during this journey of life, but we derive inspiration and strength when we know others are also going through struggles and, more importantly, when we learn how they were able to overcome them. Knowing my story could help others and their families cope with prison was more than enough incentive for me to write it. If you haven't already, I strongly encourage you to read it and get a copy for your incarcerated loved one. I have no doubt you both will come away with a renewed, reinvigorated perspective on how to bring meaning and purpose to life's most arduous circumstances — especially prison. Here is a brief synopsis of *Palpable Irony:*

> I grew up in an impoverished environment, but my parents tried their very best to shield my brother and me from the gangs, drugs, and crime that permeated our neighborhood. Despite their best efforts, we succumbed to these negative influences during our adolescent years and stole cars, smoked weed, drank alcohol, and skipped school regularly.
>
> I ended up serving over three years in prison for armed robbery when I was nineteen years old. When I was released at the age of twenty-two, I began to take my life in a new direction by attaining my GED, landing a decent-paying job, enrolling in college, and moving out of my parents' house. These successes, however, became reason for my distorted justification to drink as often as I liked without considering the consequences.
>
> On New Year's Eve, 2003, I drank and drove, and caused a devastating crash. In coming to grips with the magnitude of my addiction and what I'd done, I decided to devote my life to helping adolescents overcome addiction.

This is why I aspire to be a drug and alcohol counselor. This is why I felt compelled to make the most of this horrific situation. This is why I felt it was imperative to write the book and share how I've managed to turn a tragic circumstance into one that will ultimately have a positive outcome. And this is why I strongly feel you and your loved ones will benefit from reading *Palpable Irony.*

VALIDATION

When I got off work at 5:00 pm this evening, I immediately returned to my housing unit to check my mailbox (yes, we have those in prison) and get on the phone to call my fiancée. As I approached the phone, an associate I've known for years was coming down the tier, walking toward me. As he came within a few feet of me, he extended his hand with an inviting smile and said, "Marty, that was such a great book, man!" I knew he'd been reading my book, *Palpable Irony*, and I assumed he had just wanted to let me know he enjoyed it. I thanked him and proceeded to the phone to make my call, but this action was impeded by my friend's enthusiasm. He continued, "Man, you have no idea how much you and I have in common. For years, I've known you to be this goal-driven, educated, confident man who many guys in here look up to; but as much respect as I've had for you since I've known you, I have so much more now that I see where you came from and what you've been through." This man's touching words humbled me very much and gave me a sense of satisfaction in knowing I could reach him in this way with my story. I thanked him again for his sincere words of praise — but he was still not done.

As we stood feet from the phone I intended to use (someone else had helped themselves to it by this time, which was fine by me), he went on to tell me that he had thought for so long that some of the things he'd gone through in his life were his burdens alone, that there was "no way" other people had experienced those same things and feelings until now — now that he'd read *Palpable Irony*. Furthermore, he thanked me for, through the book, encouraging and reinvigorating him to fervently and tenaciously pursue his own passions in life. He felt my testimony was "just what he needed" to get him going again in chasing his dreams and realizing his goals.

As I intently listened to this man's passionate praise of my book and what I've been able to make of my life thus far, all I could think of was how grateful I was for moving beyond my initial trepidation of exposing my deepest flaws, and pressing forward to write the book in the hope that my brutal honesty would resonate with people — and it has. I explained to him that I was initially afraid to divulge to the public the many things in my past that I had intended to keep there, never digging them up to be relived and brought to light for all to see and judge. I was afraid of the potential castigation and judgment I would receive from those who had only known me in one way — the person I am today. I didn't want to lose credibility with those who have respected and even admired my efforts to make the most of this situation. Despite all of those very real fears, something deep inside told me if I were to lay everything on the table in my book, my readers would honor and appreciate that more than a watered-down half-truth of a story. I trusted my gut, and it paid off.

Since that memorable encounter with this man, several other inmates have read my book and the reactions from them have all echoed his. It means a great deal to know that my story has inspired and motivated men to conquer their fears, believe in themselves, and dream big for what they can still achieve, even in a seemingly meaningless situation. The fear I originally had of guys viewing me differently after reading the book has not materialized. In fact, I get the notion that because I was as honest as I was in exposing my life's adversities, flawed thinking, failures, lessons, and now triumphs, it has given me a level of credibility and influence with them that I couldn't have attained any other way. In my eyes, this is true validation.

YOU NEVER KNOW WHO'S WATCHING

When I came to prison over ten years ago, I had my mind made up that I was going to primarily keep to myself and do what I needed to do to reach my goals while avoiding getting entangled in the inevitable drama that would surround me. I started this effort by applying for a tutoring position, enrolling in college, attending church weekly, and jogging every day. I enjoyed my solitude — as much as can be expected in a prison of 1700 inmates — and was content with being somewhat sociable with a select few, but not letting anyone get "too close."

While at work one day, I noticed a young man who had just been hired to work as a tutor as well. I hadn't seen him around so I assumed he'd just arrived at the prison and wanted a high-paying prison job. Other than that initial observation, however, I didn't pay much attention to him.

I carried on with my daily regimen, conducting myself professionally while at work and respectably while not at work. Then one day (about two or three months after this young man started working in the education department) the tutor approached me at work and introduced himself, "I know we haven't met yet, but I've watched you — how you do your job, how you talk to people respectfully and don't act a fool, how you are focused on college work. I'm Sam, by the way." He went on to tell me that I reminded him a lot of his older brother who was in the military and approached everything calmly and professionally. Sam told me he was twenty-two years old and serving ten years for a DUI-related car crash that claimed the life of a mother. He seemed sincere about wanting to take his life in a new direction and was remorseful for the life he'd recklessly taken. I thought to myself, *this is a young man I believe I will enjoy getting to know*. Furthermore, I reasoned that if he had already been looking at me as an example of someone he wanted to emulate in some ways, I'd better be particularly cognizant of what I do. Of course, I wouldn't have to make any drastic changes as I was already conducting myself respectably, obviously, but *knowing* I was being paid attention to meant something to me. Granted, I knew he was not my personal responsibility, but I also believe some people cross our paths in life for a reason. It has turned out this young man would become one of my best friends.

He transferred here to the prison I'm currently at over three years ago and had been trying to convince me to follow ever since. When I arrived here three weeks ago, he was the first (and most excited) to greet me and help me get established. I was very pleased to find out he's now only six classes away from receiving his AA degree and has expressed an eagerness to return to society and work with organizations that go into high schools to warn kids about the dangers of drinking and driving. He has told me, "Marty, you set the blueprint for me, man. You showed me how I could make the most of this time." I do not say these things to give myself a proverbial pat on the back or try to claim the credit for this young man's success. I only mention it to say I'm glad I stayed committed to turning my own life around for the better and living in a way that reflects that because, after all, you never know who's watching.

3795 DAYS

Day 1: At the age of twenty-four, eight months, and ten days, I sat in an isolated jail cell in extreme agony having come out of a drunken fog and realizing I'd been responsible for a horrific drunk driving crash. Furthermore, I knew the law required that I spend a minimum of ten years in prison for this crime.

Day 276: After much prayer and meditation on what I was supposed to learn and gain from this tragedy, I came to the conclusion that I was meant to devote the rest of my life to counseling adolescents who struggle with substance addiction.

Day 362: I was sentenced to seventeen and a half years (day for day).

Day 426: I was hired as a GED tutor at the state prison I'd arrived at the previous month.

Day 633: I started my first college class at the prison.

Day 1448: I earned a Certificate of Human Services from Louisiana State University.

Day 2521: I received an Associate of Arts in General Studies from Indiana University.

Day 2704: I started writing Chapter One of my memoir.

Day 2983: I completed writing my memoir and titled it *Palpable Irony: Losing my freedom to find my purpose.*

Day 3641: I was awarded my Bachelor of Science in Sociology (Magna Cum Laude) from Colorado State University-Pueblo.

Day 3653: My memoir was published and made available to the public through online retail stores.

Day 3690: I began working on a Master of Science in Psychology from California Coast University.

Day 3795: I'm writing this blog with the hope that all who are reading it will understand that in order to make this most difficult circumstance work advantageously, it must begin by setting long-term goals that are broken down to short-term goals; short-term goals must then be broken down to monthly goals, which must be further reduced to weekly goals; and finally, weekly goals are streamlined to daily goals. This has been the key to my success and attainment of the goals I've set for myself and chronicled here. Had I simply conjured and hoped for the abstract, seemingly unattainable aspirations of becoming a counselor and publishing a book without first structuring them (my goals) the way I did, I'd be 3795 days into my sentence and still hoping to make something of my time.

It's been relatively easy to make sure I'm meeting my daily goals that keep me on pace to meet my long-term goals because I know that's all I should focus on for that day. I do not focus my attention on what I need to do for the next two or three years; this would be too overwhelming. Having said that, my long-term goal is to complete my MS degree by Day 4425! And today I did what I needed to do to keep on pace with that — I read one chapter in my textbook.

If I may offer any advice to any of you who are supporting a loved one who is incarcerated, it is to encourage him or her to strictly focus on doing something constructive for *one* day at a time! It's like the old saying, "How do you eat an elephant?" The answer: "One bite at a time." Or in this case it would be, "How do you make the most of 3795 days in prison?" The answer: "One goal-oriented day at a time!"

A BREATH OF FRESH AIR

Today's weather was ordinary for Oregon during this time of year — mild temperature, somewhat overcast, 5-10 mph wind. As I made my way down the fifty-foot concrete walkway that leads to the yard, I appreciated the fresh air and ability to get some reprieve from the confines of living in a cramped cell and crowded pod all day.

When I entered the yard area, nothing struck me as being different than any other day in prison: guys predictably walked or jogged around the track, while others vigorously pumped iron with their shirts off that revealed their chiseled, tattooed bulging muscles. The many tables that are densely positioned in one area were occupied by racially segregated or gang-affiliated occupants who played cards, dominoes, and bantered with one another. The row of fifteen phone booths were filled with eager inmates who had awaited this time all day to talk to loved ones, while thirty to forty other inmates waited feet away for their turn. As I stated, it was an ordinary day at any Oregon prison — until minutes later.

As I walked the track by myself, hoping to be left alone to listen to the eclectic music on my mp3 player, I was quickly greeted — or interrupted — by a young man who felt the need to express his admiration of my limited edition watch I'd bought at my previous prison. I thought I could just thank him for admiring my wristwatch and nonverbally convey to him that I preferred to be left alone by continuing to listen to my music as he spoke, but he didn't take the hint. Sensing I was not going to be able to peacefully listen to my music as he continued to engage me in conversation beyond the admiration of my watch, I turned off my music and we ended up conversing on a multitude of topics that, as it turned out, left me impressed and grateful for our encounter.

This young man, I learned, was only twenty-three years old and had been sentenced to fifteen years for shooting someone. He had belonged to a well-known Compton California gang (he hesitantly pointed out his gang tattoos while telling me this) and had experienced more unspeakable things than most gang members his age. But this young man's demeanor, speech, attitude, perspective on life, and intellect defied his age, intimidating physical image and gang-affiliated background. He eagerly opened up to me about how he had made the conscious, yet very difficult, decision to distance himself from his gang and instead pursue the electrician apprenticeship offered here, while sending half of his earnings home for his children; he vowed he would not be influenced by his gang affiliates to engage in destructive behavior that would certainly conflict with these goals. He spoke of how he believes God is trying to work on him and how he understands it won't happen overnight, but if he stays committed, he will do himself well over the next decade of his incarceration.

I did my best to encourage and praise him as much as I could, but he was so precocious and clearly already on the right track that I didn't feel like it was necessary to do much else but listen; so that's exactly what I did. He had to soon return to work so we couldn't talk much longer, but when we left each other I assured him we would get together and talk more.

I came away feeling blessed that God put this young man in my path today. It is moments like these that reaffirm why I came to this prison and that I'm right where I'm supposed to be, doing exactly what I'm supposed to be doing, and that *nothing* happens by accident. This young man made my ordinary day anything but. He turned out to be my true breath of fresh air today.

THE COMMUNITY CARES

I entered the air-conditioned, carpeted room that reminded me of fond memories of time spent with my family. Indeed, I'd entered the visiting room; only this time my family would not be joining me there. Instead, the visiting room tonight held an audience of sixty to seventy inmates of all ages and races who were gathered to listen to three guest speakers from the community who had been invited by the prison's Weusi Umoja African American club.

I took my seat in the front row — partly because most seats had already been taken and also because I preferred to have a good view of the speakers — and waited patiently for the meeting to begin. Moments later the club's board members (inmates) took the stage and began to briefly speak about recent developments within the club and announced what events were on the horizon. After briefing the crowd, the club president introduced the first speaker of the evening.

The speaker was a middle-aged woman who has worked with cultural clubs at other prisons in Oregon and encouraged our club to stay connected with the community. She stressed the importance of this because it would allow for long-term bonds to be built with people on the outside who can help us with our transition back into society once we are eventually released. She did not speak for a long duration, but she offered insightful knowledge that will help the club flourish from both within the prison setting and in the community for years to come.

The next speaker was a man who had walked in our shoes. He spent, in totality (through three separate sentences), approximately twenty-five of his forty-seven years on earth behind bars. He's now been out for several years, has acquired a BA in Sociology, and is currently pursuing a master's degree in Crisis Counseling from the

University of Oregon. He grew up in my neighborhood, hung out with gang members, and has participated in more crime than I have space to write here. Yet, this man has now, obviously, made a commitment to a new approach to life, which involves devoting his time to reaching out to young gang members who find themselves headed down the same troubled path. He does public speaking at his university as well as the local community college, and he travels to jails and prisons across the state to tell his harrowing story of hope and redemption. His underlying message to us tonight was about how he became driven by love and seeking a spiritual (not religious) awakening during his last prison sentence, which compelled him to make the pivotal transition that has ultimately led to the impactful work he does today.

The last guest speaker was, in my opinion, the most compelling and captivating of the evening. He was probably nearing sixty years of age and spoke with a pastor's vigor but a street hustler's grit. His message came from a deep, painful place that, no doubt, resonated throughout that packed room. He spoke of his dark days of running the streets, selling drugs, not having his father around and how that embedded in him immense pain, especially, as he later found out, after discovering that his dad lived mere blocks away from him all those years and never bothered to have a relationship with him. He was filled with emotion and unbridled passion as he spoke of how his heavy burden of pain from not having his father's love and presence drove him into a life of anger that, eventually, also led him to prison.

He now has also made it his life's mission to do community outreach as a way to connect with men and help them become better fathers to their children. He speaks in prisons and networks with several non-profit organizations to encourage and show men how to become the fathers they want to be — the fathers many of them never had. He took his pain and has used it as his driving force to encourage men to be better fathers to their children when they leave prison.

I came away from this riveting meeting with a deep sense of hope and inspiration. To see men who have walked in my shoes use this dark circumstance of prison to find enlightenment and self-motivation to help change their communities is nothing short of uplifting and praiseworthy. These men certainly motivated me to stay on the right path and return to my community to make an impact as well. It's a blessing to have community members who will volunteer their time to come in and express care and concern for those of us who need to hear an encouraging word every now and then. It's nice to see the community still cares.

CHOICES, CHANCES, CHANGES

We all have choices in life. We make countless choices on a daily basis. We can choose to go to work or stay home; wear jeans or slacks; comb our hair or wear a ball cap instead. Of course, these are some of the more mundane, trivial choices we make, but the process that leads to making even these small choices are derived from some of the same mechanisms we rely on to make more important, consequential decisions. I'd like to speak about how these choices lead to changes, which will often dictate our chances (or the lack thereof) in life.

I'm now in my fourteenth year of incarceration and have had ample time to reflect on and analyze my thought processes and subsequent behavior both before and during my incarceration. Through this critical and somewhat painstaking process, I have learned that the most determinant aspect of one's outcome in life is not just in the choices they make but, more importantly, in the motives behind their choices.

For most of us who are here, we primarily relied on a faulty rationale to justify the choices we made. Often, we made decisions based on selfishness, shortsightedness, and instant gratification. We didn't appreciate the long-term reward offered by making more productive decisions that were before us. Now we are living with the painful result of our choices. The reasons we used to justify our choices that led us here no longer make sense. Therefore, the only logical conclusion to draw from this is it would behoove us to reassess our thinking process and always consider every possible consequence to the choices we make going forward.

I have had the time to discover that for true, sustainable change to manifest, it must be catalyzed by a commitment to making constructive choices on a regular basis. Our choices, when strung together over time, formulate our habits; and good habits generally create life opportunities that will lead to the type of life we desire to lead once released from prison. But the work starts now!

Prison, as you can imagine, can be spent in a multitude of ways — most of them not productive. Again, it comes back to the motives that influence our decision making. Because I want to be a positive influence on younger guys here, I make the choice to conduct myself in a way that reflects that. I *choose* to not cuss when I speak, refer to them by their real name (not their gang moniker), and refuse to glorify past destructive behavior. My conduct must match what I "preach." The changes we make are only credible and influential when they are consistent. No one finds credible someone who vacillates in his or her conduct.

Finally, the culmination of our habitual choices that serve as evidence of our change in character will lead to greater chances in the future. When I came into this situation over twelve years ago, I had a GED. There's no shame in that accomplishment, but I knew if I was going to achieve my goal of professionally counseling those who are on a destructive path, I'd need a higher education. My formal education has resulted in degrees that will inevitably enable me to live a more fruitful, successful life when I get out. Even within these prison walls I have greater access to jobs and incentive-level housing that offers luxuries not afforded to inmates housed in other units. Aside from a formal education, simply changing the way we interact with people and carry ourselves is correlated with greater success in life.

Many variables go into influencing our decision-making process, but what I have been able to most appreciate about prison is that the many distractions that inhibited my growth before prison are gone. If one wants to take his or her life in a new direction, this is the place to do it. With all the inherent challenges prison poses, it also offers a unique opportunity to scrutinize your inner-self, perhaps like no other setting can. It all starts with analyzing our choices and the motives/

rationale behind them. It then demands a commitment to change that requires making sound, goal-oriented decisions on a regular basis. This will inevitably lead to greater chances and opportunities in life to atone for one's earlier transgressions and harms to society. Therefore, we all ought to encourage our loved ones to carefully consider their choices, make the necessary changes, and ultimately give themselves greater chances.

BEHIND THE MASK

Thank God for the many volunteers across the country who devote countless hours to traveling and helping inmates behind prison walls. We have a remarkable one here who recently started a support group for parents and grandparents who have lost children or grandchildren. The official name of this group is *The Compassionate Friends* (a renowned national organization). Unfortunately, I became a member of this contingent in 1997 when I lost my eleven-month-old son, but I can say the cathartic experience of this group today – nineteen years later – has given me a measure of strength and support that had eluded me in all the years since his passing.

There are only seven of us (including the volunteer) who meet once a week for one and a half hours to discuss both the fond and painful memories of those we have lost. We meet in the chapel where we are secluded from the housing units and general population, allowing us privacy and serenity not otherwise offered in prison. It's extremely refreshing to be in such a peaceful, quiet, and surprisingly comfortable setting within these walls. Perhaps it is the assurance of knowing there are others who share in my unfortunate loss that brings me a greater level of comfort – I'm not sure, but I appreciate and cherish it. Because we share our very solemn personal stories of how we lost our children, emotions run very high. But the beauty of this meeting is that men who are otherwise forced to wear a mask of toughness and carry an air of bravado daily can finally feel free to be vulnerable, honest, and thoughtful. Napkins are regularly passed around the table to help us through our toughest, most poignant moments. But we know we are among friends and supporters, people who share our sorrow and will not judge us when we break down and show raw pain. I cannot illustrate how powerful those moments are — you'd have to be there to witness it – but it is palpable. In fact, one member —perhaps the most stoic one of us all – managed to say through his streaming tears, "Man, it's just nice to be able to cry . . . I don't get to do it very much in here." Indeed, prison does not "allow" for this type of vulnerability for obvious reasons, so to say that this group is critically important is a gross understatement!

The stark reality of prison was soon felt once the group ended and we all headed back to our respective housing units. As we filed out into the corridor, the tears were immediately wiped away and demeanors were instantly transformed to those more conducive to both social and physical survival in this setting. There was no more talk of lost children, pain, or unanswered questions that parents of deceased children are fraught with for the rest of their lives. As much as I would have loved to carry on our painstaking conversations outside of the group (with those who are a part of the group, of course), I know it's just not going to happen, and that's okay; again, thank God for volunteers like ours who create safe havens like these, making such rare opportunities available for people who need them the most.

For me personally, perhaps the number one take away from these groups has been for me to remember that there are people all around me who carry burdens of immense grief and unexplored pain from having lost family members — children no less — or suffered other unspeakable trauma. Behind the tough exteriors and masks of indestructibility are men who hurt for many reasons and simply need an avenue — a safe haven if you will – to freely and safely express this grief. No one (inmate or not) should have to carry such heavy burdens and have no one to talk to and lean on when they need it the most. How inhuman!

I will concede that the tattoos and long beards can look scary. The stone-faced demeanors that refuse to crack a smile, even when provoked, can be quite intimidating. But before we judge, we need to keep in mind there are human beings behind those masks. And I would venture to say that nine times out of ten, when that person feels it's okay to remove the mask – even if only for an hour and a half a week — there is a hurting person who simply needs someone to lean on.

IT STARTS WITH AN EDUCATION

I have been fortunate to have the greatest job offered within the confines of prison for over ten years now as an education tutor. I'm being completely honest when I say I have enjoyed nearly every single day of it. Case in point is what has happened within the last two weeks.

The past couple weeks of my job have been especially rewarding as I've been working one on one with a couple of individuals on various subjects within the GED curriculum; they were able to enjoy the fruits of their labor by week's end. One of the young men was scheduled to be released in three weeks when I started working with him and still needed to complete three of the four required tests. He was a natural jokester who enjoyed deviating from his studies to become the center of attention, which subsequently drew others off task. Time and again I'd bring his attention back to studying, reminding him of the urgency of the task at hand, since he had only a short time to get it done. After he passed another test, he seemed to find a self-sustaining ability to focus on his studies. With only two weeks left on his sentence and two tests remaining, he became more determined than I had ever seen him.

The day before this young man was released, he completed his final two tests and graduated with his GED. He returned to the classroom after having just received his final score from the testing center, grinning from ear to ear! I learned of his success before he spotted me, but he was all too eager to proudly exclaim his achievement to the tutors: *"I passed! I got my GED!"* I went to shake his hand but he bypassed my extended hand and went in for a hug. I congratulated him, praised his hard work, and encouraged him to continue to work hard when he got out the next morning. I felt it was imperative that he absorb the magnitude of that moment, so I told him, "Listen, you can do anything you set your mind to. Let this be the evidence that shows you when you set goals for yourself and stick to them, good things are bound to happen. Let this just be the beginning of your success, young man, okay?" He listened and agreed.

Another man I've been working with has struggled mightily with a learning disability. Math has not been easy for him, not by any stretch. When we felt like he was making progress, he would test his knowledge by taking a practice test and find himself dejected when his score came back and didn't seem to reflect his ability. To say he was frustrated would be an understatement. I felt his pain because I knew he was trying with everything in him. I did my best to be the support he needed, assuring him that we would get there as long as he didn't give up. He did not.

I'm more than proud to say he finally passed his math test last week. Not only did he pass but he scored very well! He returned to the room ecstatic, hugging everyone in his path. He sought me out and I gave him a hug, telling him how proud of him I was and how much I appreciated him not giving up, despite his obstacles along the way. In his jubilation he told me, "Man, if we weren't in prison, I'd probably give you a kiss." Clearly, he was beside himself in excitement. But who could blame him? I relished the moment, reminding him of all the times he wanted to give up but didn't, again using the moment as a teachable lesson and testament to what can happen when we apply ourselves and don't succumb to doubt and frustration that can seem overwhelming at times.

I have learned through my many years of tutoring that many men who end up in prison didn't have great experiences in high school. They significantly lack confidence in their academic ability — with good reason — because, unfortunately, they didn't get the proper attention and remedial help they needed when they were in school. I don't say these things to criticize the public-school system but to merely point out a fact. My point is that it is truly an amazing thing to witness the confidence these men gain as they diligently work their way through this revamped, rigorous GED curriculum, proving to themselves along the way how capable they are when they simply apply themselves and have someone nearby who supports their efforts. The reason I appreciate it so much is I was *just* like them. When I got my GED nearly sixteen years ago, it was all the evidence I needed to convince myself that I could do more, that my greatest accomplishments lay ahead. I have no doubt the same thing is happening within each man I've had the privilege of working with over the years to earn their GED.

COMPASSIONATE CRIMINALS

I highly doubt that many people would associate the word compassion with criminal — what a paradox! After all, people are not in prison for committing random acts of kindness. No, we are here for doing just the opposite: victimizing people and leaving immeasurable damage and psychological scars in the aftermath. But what if I told you some of the most selfless acts of altruism occur right here in prison? What would you say if I told you there are men in prison who volunteer their time for no other reason than to help those who can't help themselves during their last days feel some sense of comfort and dignity before they leave this earth? Yes, I'm talking about the inmate hospice program.

Years ago, I was invited to participate in the inmate hospice volunteer program. I was surprised to learn that such a thing even existed. However, I declined the offer because, well, I was afraid. I was afraid to be that close to death. Nonetheless, I was intrigued and asked the man (an inmate) who offered me the position for a briefing on the program.

He informed me that there were six inmate volunteers who had been trained in hospice care by medical staff. Each inmate was assigned to care for one inmate at a time to ensure that each hospice patient received proper attention and care.

Duties included getting their meals, helping to dress and feed those who needed it, assisting them to the shower, phone, and their bed. But the most critical aspect of their job, he told me, was to be a good friend to these men; to listen to them, sit by their bedside, tell them stories, read to them, and simply comfort them as they battled each

MY PRISON LIFE

remaining day of their lives. The man giving me all this information was one of the longest standing volunteers in the program, and serving a life sentence — not 25 to life, but life without parole! I wondered what compelled him to devote so much of his time to nurture and care for men who wouldn't be around much longer, who weren't even his friends. Thankfully, he spared me having to ask. He told me plainly, "I'd hope someone would do it for me." Just like that.

Recently, another man told his story of being a volunteer in the hospice program. He is also serving a life sentence and has been incarcerated for nearly 30 years. Most people would justifiably assume this man has either done something heinous to receive that amount of time or, if not, would certainly be one of the most hardened, discompassionate criminals in the system after having served that much time. The former I am not privy to; and he is certainly not a hardened criminal. What he is, however, is a man who believes that helping people who can't help themselves is the right thing to do. But back to his story.

He told us (a college class) how he had taken care of a young man in hospice who suffered from a disease that had ravaged his body and would soon end his life. The young man's family sought a pardon from the governor under a provision that allows a terminally ill inmate early release, to pass away at home with family. Relieved when the Department of Corrections agreed to this petition, with the governor ready and willing to sign off on it, the inmate hospice worker shared the news with his friend that he would soon be released to be with his family. But this was not what happened. It turned out that as soon as his victim's mother was informed of his release, she vociferously protested to the governor, essentially forcing a reversal of the pardon. She wanted this young man's family to suffer the way she did when her son was killed. Her wish was granted, and his family suffered the death of their loved one while he remained incarcerated.

The inmate who gave this account choked up as he recalled his heart-wrenching experience. Clearly, this affected him in a profound way. How could it not? He cared for this young man while on his deathbed and thought he would be able to be with his family in those final precious days, hours, and minutes. I'm not going to comment on the morality or justifiability of the pained mother's protest to deny this man the comfort of being with his family in his last days — I have no place. I will just say that had it not been for the sacrifice and good will of his inmate hospice volunteer, the young man would have left this earth having been denied the most essential need we all have: the comfort of human compassion.

SIMPLY HUMAN

This past Good Friday I volunteered to work in the visiting room. I'd been asked — along with several others — to man the table set up with freshly brewed coffee, assorted flavors of creamer, sugar, tea, instant cocoa, and all the utensils needed to prepare the beverages. Visitors and their inmate loved ones could stop by the table and help themselves to what we had to offer.

Kids giggled as they walked up to the table because sitting behind it were two muscle-bound inmates ironically wearing fluffy yellow bunny ears atop their heads. Yes, I wore the silly ears! But I reasoned that this was the "lesser of two evils" since another one of us had to dress up in a full white bunny suit — head and all! But he did it and the kids loved it!

The big bunny made his way around the visiting room (led by me because apparently the suit didn't have eye openings), handing out Easter baskets full of goodies — an assortment of chocolate and marshmallow bunnies and Nestle Crunch eggs — to the many children that were there to visit their fathers, uncles, and brothers. One little girl, who couldn't have been more than a year old, clung to her daddy (an inmate) as she couldn't decide whether to be terrified of the bunny or ecstatic that he was so close to her. She shrilled one second and laughed uncontrollably the next as the bunny entertained her. Indeed, this was the highlight of my time in the visiting room that day. This little girl was simply enjoying her interaction with the giant bunny, oblivious to the environment she was in or the people it harbored. All that mattered to her for those few precious moments was that my friend was in his bunny costume. It was refreshing, innocent, and human — things I don't get the privilege to encounter every day.

It's worth mentioning that *all* funds used to purchase the items for the visitors to enjoy (the entire week) came from inmate donations! All monies used to purchase the items inside the baskets and the baskets themselves came from inmate fundraisers conducted over the past several months. Furthermore, each visitor who had a small child could take a free picture — also paid for by inmate contributions.

The actual facilitating, planning, purchasing, and orchestration of this event was done by The La Raza Club — one of several inmate cultural clubs that are composed of and run by inmates. Each major ethnic group (and Lifers) has a club that raises money and sponsors events for all inmates to enjoy throughout the year. This Easter celebration for inmates and their families and loved ones is but one of several that was made possible through the efforts of these clubs and their fundraisers. Fundraisers are also planned and executed entirely by inmate board members from the respective clubs. Items for purchase generally consist of various food items that are otherwise not available to us (i.e., Papa Murphy's pizza, chicken strips, barbecue ribs, etc.). As you can imagine, inmates are all too eager to contribute to these fundraisers as they offer a two-fold reward.

I volunteered for both morning and afternoon visiting sessions on Friday, and barely realized I had spent six hours there. The atmosphere was a stark contrast to what I'm used to; small children have a way of softening their environment. Parents and grandparents approached our table throughout their visiting sessions just to pour a cup of hot coffee and tell us how much they appreciated what we were doing. I cannot express how much it meant to hear someone wearing civilian clothes tell us they were grateful for what we'd done. That's not been an exchange I've had in many years. Again, it was a simple, yet profound moment of humanity. In fact, everything that happened on Friday was simply human — there's no other way to describe it.

PART III

Maintaining Romance
Beyond the Bars

SHE'S 'DOING TIME' TOO

I recently heard another inmate on the phone next to me berate who was presumably his girlfriend on the other end of his line. Soon after she accepted his call he began to scold her over numerous things he felt she should be doing for him. I heard him yell into the receiver, "You're not the one doing the time — I am!" Granted, I don't know this man's situation or the extent of his relationship with this woman, but it compelled me to think about the sacrifices that women make to show their devotion to their relationships. It didn't take much time for me to staunchly disagree with his assertion that she's not doing time — only he is. In fact, I thought, women who stand by men in prison *are*, in a sense, "doing time" too.

True enough, my fiancée can come and go as she pleases throughout her day, but she is also subject to the time constraints imposed on her by my imprisonment when it comes to the limited opportunities that we are able to communicate. She has been forced to alter her schedule to accommodate our calls, look things up for me via the internet, and, yes, fly over 2,500 miles twice a year to visit me.

Sure, she can eat whatever and whenever she prefers, but how often does she wish she could sit down to enjoy a meal with me? How often does she feel like crying inside as she walks past a restaurant and glances through the large windows to witness other couples enjoying lunch together, wishing with everything in her that could be us?

That disgruntled inmate on the phone next to me might have made the flimsy case that his girlfriend was not physically doing time because she can sleep in her own bed every night — a spacious, soft, comfortable bed, no less. However, my rebuttal to this shortsighted argument would be although she can enjoy this freedom, she is also left with a huge void as she tosses and turns night after night in mental anguish because she desperately desires to finally be held in her man's loving arms again. Her soul grieves as she can only imagine being engulfed in the safety and comfort of his strong arms while she sleeps in her comfortable bed. How many nights have there been where she lay in sleepless agony while longing for the day she can share her bed with the one person in the world she wishes to?

A lot of men in prison fail to place themselves in others' shoes when it comes to grasping the impact of this situation as it is felt by those who love and support us. They fail to do this because, largely, they are self-centered and expect everyone to feel sorry for them. They erroneously believe they are the *only* ones truly affected by their long absence because, after all, they'll reason, they are the ones who are physically confined. I have been in a relationship and in the company of many other men in healthy relationships long enough to know this is categorically false.

Just as we inmates eagerly long for and anticipate the glorious day when we are set free from captivity, so do the women and men who stand by and support us every step of the way. Just as we continually daydream about doing the simple things in life with our loved ones — going out to eat, grocery shopping, walking in the park, for instance — so do they! Knowing this then, it's virtually impossible to make the offensive claim that she's not doing time too.

COMMUNICATION IS THE KEY

From the moment we are born, we want to be heard. No — we demand it! We emerge from our mothers screaming and crying until we are quickly wrapped in a soft blanket and held against the warm, comforting body of our primary caregiver.

As we grow, we continue to cry out in an effort to be held, receive food when hungry, and be rocked to sleep when tired. We innately make the connection from infancy that when we make noise, we will be heard and, subsequently, our needs will be met.

As we develop into toddlers, young children, adolescents, and adults, we rely on more sophisticated tactics to get people to pay attention to our needs, to be heard. Some of these strategies are less constructive than others in the long run, but we will nonetheless repeat any behavior that yields results that we ultimately desire. So if the silent treatment (albeit unhealthy) makes someone pay attention to our disgruntled mood and thus causes him or her to respond to our need, we will likely continue this behavior.

I highlight these points to say that our central desire to be heard and have our needs met don't ever leave us. Subsequently, when we enter relationships, we want nothing more than to have the person we're with listen to us, show empathy and understanding, and reciprocate these forms of communication and compassion. And this, in my opinion, is why many relationships in which a woman is supporting her man in prison thrive as well as they do.

For many men in general, the ability to express one's feelings when communicating is not as easy as it is for most women. Society, peers, and upbringing all factor in to why men find it very difficult to easily express themselves while listening to women they are in relationships with. But when a man comes to prison and his need for love and companionship become more pronounced, he begins to understand the importance of effectively communicating with his partner.

Because he is only able to express his love through the limited means available in prison (i.e. verbal and written communication), he hones these skills and becomes more adept over the course of his incarceration. His significant other has her needs met through his emotional maturity because he can finally give her the attentiveness she desires. His ability to actively listen and openly communicate assures her that he sincerely cares about her.

Many people will readily admit that communication is vital in any relationship, yet they don't necessarily know what it means to carry this out. For me, I had to learn over time that when my fiancée vents about certain things, she is not necessarily expecting me to "fix" it for her; she merely wants me to listen. This took some adjustment for me because I, as many men do, have always thought of myself as a natural problem solver. But in order to become a good listener and someone who is attentive to his fiancée's needs, I had to adjust my approach.

In any relationship, we desire to be heard and have our feelings validated and appreciated, so it's no wonder that many women in committed relationships with men in prison find so much satisfaction and fulfillment that others don't always understand — he has the time to listen to her. His learned ability to effectively communicate with her has ultimately turned out to be the key to her heart.

BEND BUT DON'T BREAK

Inmates and their families and friends experience a range of emotions regarding the difficulty of their situation. For many of us who are incarcerated, we are forced to adapt to the confines of prison and find creative ways to form a semblance of normalcy in our daily routines. But even though we settle in and accept our new way of living, we still go through periods of emotional anguish and even depression. Some days just have a way of beating you down.

Mental fortitude is what humans rely on to overcome demanding situations. To continually fight against things that are out of our control would only exhaust and frustrate us, so we accept our unchangeable fate to successfully navigate whatever obstacles are before us. Because I am in a committed relationship, I also know prison can be equally difficult and emotionally taxing for the women who stand by us through this tumultuous hardship.

I have profound respect and admiration for the mental tenacity of women (especially mothers) who manage busy lives while simultaneously caring for a man in prison. She accommodates him, the children, and God knows who else, all because she loves him and knows there are people who mightily depend on her. She holds it all together in view of the public because strength is what she embodies and doesn't want anyone to spend any time worrying about her, but she is only human and has her moments when the pain and agony of it all gets the best of her — how could it not? I suspect there has been many a night when she has put the kids to bed, let her hair down, and had a good ol' fashioned cry because she misses her man (or son) more than words can express.

NOT LOOKING BACK

Our past is like an old scar on a part of our bodies that is usually covered by our clothing. In other words, it's not prominent in our lives but it is still there when we're bare. If you are like me, you don't particularly like it when people remind you of some aspects of your past. For many of us, these represent things either painful or shameful and, as far as we're concerned, are better off remaining in our "forgotten" past.

When I came to prison, I lived with the burden of knowing I was responsible for my costly decision to drink and drive. Added to that was the guilt and regret I carried after realizing how badly I treated my then-girlfriend during the entire two years of our relationship. Contemplating these issues caused me psychological and emotional distress. However, after much self-reflection and continual prayer, I began to see not just the futility in this negative thinking but the sheer detriment this insidious mindset was having on my ability to be productive, to use this situation for development. I came to understand the same energy I was putting into this negative thinking could be rechanneled into positive progress and growth.

When I entered the relationship I'm currently in, I learned that true love of self and the person you're with means you do not badger them about their past. You do not bring up their past mistakes and imperfections when you disagree on things. I came to understand that forcing someone to relive his or her past only prevents the possibility of progress for the relationship going forward. It's just not productive for either of you.

A loving relationship, I've learned, is one where both parties can look beyond their partner's mistakes and instead appreciate the many qualities they possess now. This is clearly what my fiancée saw in me when she took the initiative to write to me, despite my circumstance. Honestly, when I came to prison with over seventeen years on my sentence and my then-girlfriend having recently left me, I had no reason to believe a woman would be interested in a romantic relationship with a man in my shoes. Many people, rightfully so, frown heavily upon drunk drivers, so I knew this could be a hindrance to me finding a meaningful relationship. Furthermore, I internalized this shame and believed, to an extent, that I was not worthy of having someone in my corner the way she has been. Thank God, my fiancée did not see it this way.

We both have been able to focus on and appreciate what our relationship is because we refuse to look back into each other's lives and dredge up the past as we know this would only inhibit us from moving forward. We have become a very strong couple because we accept each other's flaws, yet we don't allow them to define us or dictate our course of action going forward. We choose to remain focused on the present while remaining optimistic about our future. Neither of us can rewrite our pasts, so why revisit them? What possible good can come from doing so? Okay, let me rephrase that: revisit the past only to highlight a lesson learned, but don't live there. Acknowledge it, sure, but then move on and put that energy into the growth of the relationship, otherwise there will be no relationship.

I'm grateful for having such a forgiving, compassionate woman in my life who does not judge me on my past failures but who instead chooses to look at who I am and what I want to be and do today. Any relationship that stands a chance of persevering through this extremely difficult circumstance requires a conscious effort on the part of both parties to appreciate and live in the present.

WHY WOMEN LOVE BAD BOYS

For many gentle, outgoing, emotionally intelligent men, it is most frustrating when they see many of the women they take an interest in throw themselves at the tattooed, mean-mugging, tank-top-wearing guy who doesn't appear to be going anywhere in life. His insecurities cause him to question if he is less of a man because he's more comfortable wearing khakis and polo shirts than dingy jeans, white tank-top undergarments as shirts, and unlaced work boots on a regular basis. He knows he is a good guy with a big heart and is attentive to a woman's needs, but he feels he is not what women want because, after all, it is the guy who is opposite him in every feasible way that attracts women he's interested in.

Prison is rife with men who attract women who have "a thing" for men who project an image of thuggery and hyper-masculinity. Some women enthusiastically scour prison pen pal websites in an effort to meet their insatiable need of finding the ultimate bad boy. They will write to him, visit him, send him money and likely fall head over heels, not with *him*, but with the image he projects. In all actuality, this infatuation precludes a woman from truly knowing him because she is so enamored with what he appears to be that she fails to perceive that his facade is so thick he doesn't let anyone in close enough to *really* get to know him. Yet, in spite of this reality, she remains attracted to him. What compels her to turn down men who are responsible, mature, hardworking, family-oriented, and emotionally available for the men who are detached, hardened, and not interested in meeting her core needs?

Women are nurturers. Therefore, it is understandable that they would be inclined to believe that given the proper amount of love and nurturing they can provide to the hardened individual, he will transform into a more vulnerable, loving, expressive person who will in turn meet her emotional needs. In her mind, it is especially gratifying to be the catalyst for such a radical transformation, to develop this "project" to its ideal end. The tough exterior of the rough-riding bad boy intrigues and entices her to "save him." And this would be mistake number one!

Another compelling reason women are drawn to these types of men is because they represent her ideal of true masculinity. They outwardly appear to be tough enough to defend, protect (her and her children), and even put her in her place when she needs it. They represent, in her mind, the essential core of what constitutes a man. However, in *only* seeing these traits, while overlooking many others, she inevitably sets herself up for severe disappointment.

She is attracted to his rough-edged persona, yet she implores him to show some compassion and be there for her emotionally when she is going through a crisis. She is intrigued with his nonchalant demeanor, yet she wishes he would be more proactive with their kids' activities and homework. Again, she became so fixated on the idea of him but failed to genuinely get to know him. Had she done so, she may have thought twice about investing so much of her time, money, and emotions in their relationship in the first place.

This assertion is not to declare that anyone who looks the part is a bad candidate for a relationship, but it's critical when selecting a potential mate that we evaluate every aspect of *why* we are drawn to a person. For women who are especially fascinated with bad boys and looking to date an inmate who projects this persona, be prepared to get the full-on bad boy — not just the image.

ARE YOU ASKING OR DEMANDING?

When we lose control of situations, we often look for ways to immediately regain control through forceful or tactical measures. For instance, parents will find that certain punishments (i.e. restricting their kids' television hours or taking their iPod) are no longer effective as their kids get older and continue to disobey them. Feeling a sense of helplessness, the parents will turn to more severe forms of punishment (i.e. cancelling their driver's license or calling the police if their behavior is harmful to anyone in the household) to curb their behavior. This is an innate human reaction when we are faced with anxiety-provoking circumstances that result in a sense of a loss of control. This is something I have especially noticed in prison.

When I came to prison, I clung to my then-girlfriend by expecting unreasonable obedience to my needs and desires. I was manipulating her to get what I wanted. I would, for instance, demand — not ask — that she put money on my account so I could purchase canteen items, add money to the phone account for us to talk regularly, and come visit me routinely to "show her love" to me. Like many men, I would make my "requests" by starting with the cliché line, "If you really love me," when this was nothing less than a crafty attempt to regain a sense of control over a situation that, in actuality, I no longer had control of.

Throughout my incarceration, I've noticed I was not alone in this regard. Many men resort to using such tactics to feel as though they still maintain some level of influence over their girlfriend's/wife's behavior. However, having now come to understand the impetus behind this kind of manipulation, I can readily admit that I am in no position to make demands of anyone, nor is this reflective of a mutually loving and respectful relationship. Moreover, I have learned when people do things because they feel forced to, they begin to build and harbor resentment toward the person making those demands. And resentment that goes unchecked for long enough can only result in one way — badly.

Today, I'm pleased to say I share a give-and-take relationship with my fiancée. I have come to discover that it feels incredibly rewarding to freely give what I can offer while receiving her kind acts of love in return. I know my fiancée's attention and service to my needs are solely because she loves me and genuinely wants to see me succeed in life after prison, not because she feels obligated.

Our relationship, as well as countless others', thrives in large part because there is a mutual exchange in what we offer and receive from each other. We gladly give each other what we can for no other reason than we love and want to help each other in any way we are able to. No demands. No manipulation.

My advice to anyone (especially my incarcerated brethren) who uses manipulation to control his or her partner ought to understand you're only doing your relationship a disservice in the long run. The next time you want your partner to do something for you, try asking instead of demanding — it will be received much better.

FOLLOW YOUR HEART

The true essence of what drives us lies in our heart. Our deepest passions, interests, and motives pour out from our hearts and into the world through our behaviors. Our heart is the source and origin of who we are, what we like — and dislike — and what truly fulfills our needs. This is also why when the heart is broken or malcontent, we cannot help but feel disoriented to the point of it affecting our entire mood. We are unable to function to a degree, and it takes time to return to our old selves.

Many of you in relationships with someone in prison know quite well there are many people — both family and friends — in your circle who do not approve of your relationship simply because your other half is locked up. They don't know him (or her) and have no interest in doing so. Yet, they have no qualms about expressing their ill feelings toward the relationship, often saying they believe you would be much happier if you were to separate yourself and move on with your life with someone who is not incarcerated. What they fail to realize, however, is your heart is already taken by the person you are with and, therefore, is not available for someone else to occupy. Your heart tells you that the right thing to do is stay committed to your partner because he or she makes you happy like no other has been able to or could. Your heart still flutters when your significant other calls, and it weeps when you hear the dreaded words, "You have one minute remaining," on the automated phone recording. You know that your heart would be immensely grieved if you left your significant other, especially in their greatest time of need — but many people will never understand that.

A lot of us live under the pressure of meeting the demands of others: friends, family, bosses, and society at large. Everyone seems to have a vested interest in how we live our lives, who we love, where we work, what kind of car we drive, and the list could go on. I don't have to tell you how powerful these pressures can be because you feel them daily. Therefore, it takes a self-assured, confident person to be able to combat and reject these expectations and do what makes you happy — not others! It takes courage, resolve, and commitment to be willing to sacrifice friendships and even sever family ties that have caused a great deal of stress and anxiety over your relationship with your incarcerated loved one. But this, again, is a testament to the power of conviction in your heart that tells you the person you're with is *exactly* who you are meant to be with — regardless of what others may think.

A lot of the things we instinctively feel may often conflict with our rational mind. Our heart tells us one thing while our head tells us something else, often in total contradiction to one another. Other people are only using their head, telling you that you're making a huge mistake by staying with the person you love because he or she is locked up for a long time. But if it were *their* heart involved, do you think they'd be saying the same thing? We have instincts and undeniable feelings for a reason. Often, they are meant to guide us away from potential danger or harm, but they also serve the purpose of guiding us to places we otherwise wouldn't have gone — places of fulfillment and happiness. In other words, our instincts compel us to take risks and venture to do things that allow us to flourish in ways we otherwise would have avoided out of fear. And for this reason, I will always endorse the idea that we ought to do what we feel compelled to do, disregard what others say about it, and follow our heart — it's usually right!

IT'S THE LITTLE THINGS THAT MATTER

Growing up, I was socialized to believe that a person's monetary status was synonymous with one's self-worth and value as a human being. And this, so I thought, would likewise correlate with one's level of happiness. Pretty simple: the more money you have, the happier you'll be. In pursuit of this "happiness," I sought to look the part of someone successful by obtaining the flashy car, clothes, and women; yet, my bank account reflected something entirely different.

Despite the success I did eventually achieve through working, I was not truly fulfilled in my spirit. I was confused. How was it that I had a nice car, nice clothes, a decent job, no shortage of attractive women, and yet I felt empty inside? I began to feel I had been hoodwinked by society and the media that led me to believe the material things I sought would bring me internal, sustainable happiness, yet left me feeling empty and spiritually destitute.

It wasn't until I came to prison and was stripped of those material, superficial items that I discovered what truly brings satisfaction and internal happiness that lasts day after day, month after month, and year after year was not those things but relationships. Having a woman who loves me for who I am and inspires me to be the best I can be is what brings me true happiness. Looking forward to hearing her utter "I love you" at the end of every phone call is what brings a smile to my heart. Knowing I have the rest of my life to spend with her is what fulfills my soul.

We often talk and daydream about things we envision doing together when I get out. It excites me when we talk about going to I-Hop and how I'm going to order French toast with strawberries, blueberries, scrambled eggs with cheese, sausage links, and a tall glass of fresh orange juice (with pulp, of course). I feel energized when we talk about attending church together and then going to lunch afterward to discuss the sermon.

We often talk about how awesome it will be to take one vacation a year to various states and abroad, attending a Dallas Cowboys (her first love) game together, and even taking an afternoon stroll together, holding hands, on a sunny day in the park.

These simple life pleasures that we often take for granted bring me joy when thinking about doing them with the woman I've come to love with every fiber of my being. The more I have thought about why these things bring me the joy that material things could not, I have come to understand that one of our core needs as human beings is to connect with others. Our spirit will only be fulfilled when we establish an intimate bond with someone we know and love beyond comprehension. It is no wonder that all the material things I owned left me devoid of happiness.

It doesn't thrill me to know it took coming to prison for me to finally realize that my perception and pursuits of happiness were misguided and futile, but I am eternally grateful for having had the unique opportunity to discover it is relationships — not material possessions — that have the capability of bringing about true happiness. In other words, it is the "little things" in life that truly matter.

SHE MAKES ME BETTER

If we're lucky, we will meet someone who naturally inspires us to be the absolute best version of ourselves we can be. It's not that they come into our lives with the purpose of doing that — not at all. They simply show us through their actions how much they believe in us while doing everything in their power to help us achieve our goals and reach our fullest potential. It is only by the grace of God that I've been fortunate enough to meet such a person during my darkest days.

When I embarked on this long journey over eleven years ago, I had made up my mind that I wanted to utilize this time to earn a college education and become a substance abuse counselor to adolescents. As noble as this vision was for someone in my shoes, I had absolutely no clue how, or if, I was even going to be able to attain such a goal. There were two reasons for my doubt: money and a lack of self-confidence.

College is not free, so obviously when federal Pell Grants for inmates were abolished in the 1990s, it became virtually impossible to attain a college degree for those of us behind bars. This, in part, made me believe my aspirations would remain just that. Little did I know, God had other plans. He knew what it would take for me to reach these goals and took it upon Himself to place an amazing woman in my life who would endorse everything I aspired to do to better my life. She would show her support by generously offering financial assistance as well as taking the initiative to do research and administrative paperwork required for me to enroll in a college degree program. She was more than up to the task. I was completely humbled beyond words when she fully committed herself to helping me attain my education. I promised her I would not disappoint her, that I would get good grades to show her how appreciative I was for her unmatched generosity and belief in me — and I have.

She has remained my greatest supporter since that day many years ago. Her unwavering enthusiasm radiates and influences me to believe in myself the same way she does. Whenever I begin to even slightly doubt myself about anything, she's the first one to sharply criticize this and encourage me to think positively and confidently. Where would I be without this woman?

Many men in prison have the ability and potential to make a pivotal transformation in their thinking and subsequent behavior while here. The difference, however, in the men who do and others who don't can be the presence and support of an incredible woman in their corner who motivates them to be better; a woman who believes in her man's dreams and does what she can to see them materialize is priceless.

I used to wonder — why me? Why did God bring this amazing woman into my life and offer me a bright future that has been made possible, in large part, by her commitment and love? This was when I still suffered from poor self-esteem, believing I was not worthy or deserving of such a blessing. But I don't do this to myself anymore. Because of her constant support and encouragement of my efforts, I have come to love and believe in myself. God has confirmed, through her, how deserving I am to have a meaningful life of purpose and fulfillment. I know I can continue to achieve great things in the future.

I never knew how one could truly know when they've met "the one" — their soul mate. What would "the sign" or key indicator be to signify someone is this special person? I've now come to understand in crystal clear terms how a man knows when he's met the one he is meant to spend his entire life with: she makes him better.

INTIMACY: THE OTHER KIND

Romantic relationships are comprised of three essential components: passion, commitment, and intimacy. Passion is usually most prominent in the beginning of a relationship; it is that insatiable desire to spend every waking moment with the person you're madly in love with. It is also the reason there is an immense void felt when that person is absent. Commitment is the component that sustains a relationship after that initial wave of passion has subsided; it is the unwavering sense of loyalty and honesty to each other. It is an effortless sense of obligation to each other, wherein both parties understand that when they help the other, it strengthens the relationship. Lastly, there is intimacy. This word, as you know, is perhaps a bit more complex, which is why I will focus my attention on its multifaceted meaning.

When most people hear this provocative, ambiguous term, they generally only think of its physical manifestation. And although this is certainly an important aspect of a romantic relationship, obviously, it is not the *only* form of intimacy, nor, dare I say, the *most* important! The "other kind" of intimacy is what I believe to be the most integral component needed to sustain a relationship. This form of intimacy is made up of two ingredients: self-disclosure and emotion.

Throughout our days we involuntarily have thousands of thoughts. Most of them are fleeting and somewhat meaningless, while others are more significant. It is these more meaningful thoughts, desires, aspirations and reflections that we wish to share with someone we hope will appreciate and validate them while offering their own. This form of intimacy fosters closeness and trust in a relationship. The support we receive from our partner during our most vulnerable divulgences enables us to trust and rely on their comfort when we need it the most. This closeness allows relationships to thrive in the absence of physical intimacy.

This intimate sharing has been the catalyst to the growth my fiancée and I have enjoyed throughout our relationship. It is what has allowed each of us to gladly offer the other the innermost part of who we are as individuals without fear or timidity. We do not shy away from such self-disclosures because we have come to be confident in the other's support and safety in doing so. It is this reciprocal sharing that has enabled us to know the other as well as we know ourselves. These elements working in concert have enabled us to know without hesitation that we are each other's best friend.

In prison, I've not only learned to love myself (by accepting my flaws), but through that process have also learned how to truly love a woman, accepting her imperfections as well. I have come to understand that for me to provide her with what she needs, I must first be able to look beyond myself and understand what makes her feel loved. She and I enjoy sharing our innermost thoughts, desires, concerns, and feelings with each other to further cultivate our emotional and intellectual intimacy. We come away from many of our conversations feeling mentally and emotionally stimulated.

Many people have negative, disparaging things to say about these types of relationships because, in large part, they tend to focus on the part of intimacy that is missing. They either don't understand, choose to ignore, or grossly underestimate how a woman can be truly satisfied in a relationship that lacks physical intimacy. However, what they fail to realize is that any relationship that is going to thrive and have a promising future must possess something much more substantive: otherwise known as the 'other kind' of intimacy.

BEST OF TEAMMATES

I'm an avid sports fan. I can't get enough of football (both collegiate and professional) when it is in season, and basketball gets me thoroughly excited as my Portland Trailblazers are beginning to look competitive again.

What has especially intrigued me through sports is how teammates (who have all charted their own impressive paths to reach the height of their careers) are able to work in unison to compete toward a common goal. What is also amazing, when you think about it, is how even the greatest of players (i.e. Michael Jordan, Lebron James, Joe Montana, and others) would not have been able to maximize their potential and reach professional stardom had it not been for their teammates.

This same general concept can also be applied to relationships — especially relationships of this type (where one is incarcerated) where adversity is a continuous theme throughout. And just like teammates do at the professional level, when one member of the team goes down because of an injury or otherwise and needs their teammates to step up and perform in their absence, relationships require this same amplified effort.

In my own relationship, I often refer to us as teammates, especially when she is in need of emotional support through a very difficult time; and clearly, she is my emotional support through every day of this incredibly trying period of my life. I do my best to strengthen and encourage her in her moments of pain, and she is my rock when this storm becomes more turbulent and seemingly unbearable.

Teammates can always count on each other; they complement, motivate, and remind each other, when need be, of the common goal they are working toward when either of them becomes frustrated and temporarily loses sight of it. For football players, this goal is winning the next game and eventually winning the Super Bowl; for basketball players, it is making the playoffs and working through a grueling tournament to ultimately reach The NBA Finals and hoist the Larry O' Brian trophy after the final game. For us, it is merely getting through this rigorous prison sentence with our relationships as strong as possible so we can embark on the rewarding life with our mates that we have dreamt about for years. Therefore, when times get especially hard — which happens somewhat regularly in this situation — it takes at least one half of the duo to encourage and uplift their downtrodden, discouraged teammate, to help them recommit their drive and focus toward the ultimate long-term goal.

As great as some of the most memorable teams throughout history were, they would never have been able to reach their lofty heights, enshrined in sports immortality, had it not been for their solidarity and togetherness. Their unified goal and approach is what led them to an eminent status in their respective professions; the same can be said for myself and others who strive to reach goals while in prison. I could not have accomplished half the things I have had it not been for the help of my "teammate" and best friend. She is the love of my life and the life of my love. She is my life partner and the very best teammate I could ever ask for.

WHY SHE STAYS

A woman's world can come to a screeching halt when her longtime boyfriend, fiancé, or husband has been arrested and faces serious charges that could land him in prison for many years. She will likely go through a series of emotions that will begin with frustration and confusion, which could lead to depression, despair, and immense stress until she finally accepts that he will not be returning into her loving arms anytime soon. At that juncture she is then faced with a very tough dilemma that demands a critical decision be made: does she stay or does she go?

Many of her friends will ask her, "Why would you stay?" or "Why not just leave him and start over with someone else?" Often the first words out of her mouth in response to them will be, "Because I love him." And by all accounts this should be a sufficient answer; after all, quite simply, that *is* the essence of why she stays during this period of hardship, but I would like to elaborate on this explanation if I may.

What I have learned through my relationship with my fiancée is she endures the difficulty of this situation because she finds qualities in me she has not been able to find in any other man prior to meeting me. She and I have established a connection and bond that far exceed the superficial ones we both experienced in our relationships prior to knowing each other. She stays because she understands anything worth having that is truly meaningful and fulfilling is indeed worth waiting for.

The alternative to staying is always an option, of course. She could decide to leave, meet someone else, and never contact me in the future; but what good would this do if in fact her heart is still with me? Why would she "go through the motions" of being in a relationship with someone else if she can't fully give him her heart because it's still with me?

It appears that when people suggest to these women who are standing by their incarcerated men that they should leave them and move on, they simply ignore the point I just made and don't understand or appreciate the durability and capability of true love. True love knows no boundaries, no limits, and no barriers. When you truly love someone, women in relationships with men in prison would say, you don't leave them when they need you the most. If you do, was it in fact *true* love to begin with? Or was it an as-long-as-everything-is-going-fine kind of love?

The word *love* means limitless things to many people and I will not attempt to offer a lengthy list of what I personally think it means. What I *will* say is love is inherently selfless and sacrificial. It is this aspect of love that compels a woman in this kind of relationship to stay with her man through this tumultuous time. It is this unselfish aspect of true love that enables her to disregard the naysayers and hold firm to her belief that everything she is going through to keep her relationship intact is well worth it.

We all make numerous decisions about something or another every day. Sometimes we intuitively do things because we believe they will benefit us in some way. Well, there is no question that a woman's decision to stay with her man through his lengthy sentence is very much the same. The fact that she loves him, however, is merely the beginning of why she chooses to stay.

WHY DID I GET MARRIED?

No, I'm not married, nor is this blog a reference to the renowned motion pictures produced by Hollywood actor and producer Tyler Perry. It is about the fact that countless inmates decide to commit themselves before God and witnesses in marriage to women they have trepidation about marrying and the reasons behind it. In other words, they go forward with the marriage, not because they have envisioned spending the rest of their lives with these women who fulfill their needs in every way, but because they believe doing so will ensure they will have these women's support through the duration of their sentences.

When I was in the county jail and facing nearly twenty years in prison, my then-girlfriend was my main source of comfort and stability beside my family. She came to visit me as often as she could, put money on my commissary account regularly, and sent me countless love letters and cards almost daily. She was my solace through a horrible, depressing circumstance that I put myself in. I relied on her for comfort and peace of mind.

When considering the prospect of spending the next decade or more in prison, I felt I had to do whatever I could to hold on to her. My vulnerability led me to propose to her and declare I was a "changed man" regarding my habitual cheating throughout our relationship. I convinced her I wanted nothing more than to spend the rest of my life with her, and she eagerly agreed to marry me. However, much to our dismay, the pastor we had hoped would marry us (we had to secure our own pastor) declined to do so because he said he would need to counsel us before he felt comfortable performing our marriage. Looking back on this, I am more convinced than ever that *all things* happen for a reason.

That relationship went extremely awry over the next couple years, and in the aftermath of it I met and fell in love with an amazing woman whom I've now been with for over nine years. The point of illustrating the near costly mistake of marrying my ex-girlfriend is to highlight that I almost married her out of pure desperation and vulnerability — not love and commitment. In fact, while at a visit with my then-girlfriend and my mom, my mother told me she thought I was making a huge mistake and implored me to think long and hard about what I was doing because, again, she felt like I was only agreeing to marry her because I was vulnerable. There is something about a mother's intuition.

I'm certainly not trying to discourage anyone from getting married in this situation because, after all, I don't pretend to know everyone's relationship dynamics. What I can say, however, is I have witnessed many men in here (including me) who had never thought about marrying these women until they found themselves in this predicament and needed someone to stick with them through their hardship. Many men in prison have married, gotten released, and, sadly, shortly thereafter, left the women who had invested everything they had in them. I cannot cite concrete numbers to substantiate my claim as to the vast number of people this has happened to, but I venture to say they are staggering.

Marriage is such a significant commitment made on the part of both involved, and I personally believe it would do both parties and the institution of marriage itself a service if they were to wait until he is released from prison to make it official. The reason for this is simple: it gives the couple ample time in a real-world context to determine if in fact they still feel the same way about each other after his release. The last thing either of you want to do is wake up one day and utter to yourself, "Why did I get married?"

IF ROLES WERE REVERSED

I'm amazed at how much women can endure in a relationship with a man behind bars. What they go through to show their unwavering love and commitment to their incarcerated loved one is nothing short of remarkable and admirable. The immense sacrifices they make epitomize what it means to be "all in."

Paired with the appreciation for what women endure throughout these trying circumstances is the overwhelming sense of how fortunate I am because I have a woman who has been showing her love and support for me over the course of *many* years. I can also readily admit that if roles were reversed, I would not meet the level of commitment she (and countless other women) has exhibited. In fact, I would venture to go out on a pretty sturdy limb and say *most* men who benefit from having an incredible woman in their corner during their period of incarceration would not demonstrate the same degree of commitment if the situation were reversed. Ladies, I'm sorry to say, we would collectively fail you miserably in this regard.

It is also this bleak, shameful reality that makes me not only appreciate my own relationship even more so, but also makes me incensed when I hear prisoners complain about what their girlfriend or wife hasn't done for them, as if they're obligated to drop everything they're doing to accommodate them. I want to shake them and yell, "Be grateful she's even still here because if the roles were reversed, you sure wouldn't be!"

It is this lack of empathy that partially landed many of us in prison in the first place. If we would have learned, developed, and used this kindergarten-acquired social skill of putting ourselves in others' shoes before doing what we did that led us here, I'm confident in saying things would have turned out differently for many of us; but we didn't and, sadly, many incarcerated men still don't exhibit this core trait, especially as it relates to what their girlfriends or wives go through for the sake of their relationship. Instead, they selfishly take them, and what they do, for granted.

When considering how fortunate many men are to have the tenacious support of women as they go through their lengthy sentences, I can't help but simultaneously feel sorrow for the many women who are incarcerated and have lost contact with their boyfriends or husbands and subsequently their children in many cases due to their incarceration. When I'm in a packed visiting room, witnessing dozens of women who are there visiting their men, I sometimes wonder if the visiting rooms in women's prisons look like ours. Are they full of men who are there to see them with their kids in tow? If I had to offer an educated guess, I would answer with a resounding no!

It's evident that women are much better suited than men to remain loyal through these circumstances due to the fact they are biologically designed to be driven toward establishing an emotional connection with a potential mate; while men, having these same capacities (though to a lesser degree), more prominently possess a strong biological nature driven toward physical intimacy that can operate with or without emotional attachment. I would also venture to say that myriad women who stand by their men could honestly admit to themselves that, if roles were reversed, most would not be confident in their man's ability to reciprocate her efforts. Appreciating this fact makes me understand and readily proclaim that my fiancée is undoubtedly a better woman than I am a man.

I DON'T WANNA KNOW

Many men in prison who are in relationships accept the fact that their girlfriend or wife is human and, therefore, has biological, physical impulses and desires that his situation renders him incapable of fulfilling. Some men have explicitly negotiated with their significant other their acceptance of her seeking physical pleasure with another man during his absence, as long as she does not "catch feelings" for him. Having settled for this agreement to have her continued support through his incarceration, it still pains him to know the woman he loves will give herself to another man in this intimate way. Others have discussed with their partners the potentiality of this happening in their absence, and have requested that their girlfriend or wife not tell them if, and when, it inevitably happens. These men reason that it's not their "right" to complain about it or demand that she stays faithful with her body because, after all, he can't meet her physical needs so she "needs" to find it somewhere.

Despite his acquiescence, the mere thought of his significant other sharing a passionate, intimate encounter with another man is gut-wrenching and devastating. But he tries to psychologically mitigate the anguish by telling himself if he doesn't know about it or when it happens, he can handle it. This, I believe, is a fallacy. The human brain is much smarter than that.

I know from personal experience this rationale is flawed because I reasoned with my former girlfriend that I could handle it if I didn't know when she slept with another man. Yet, every time I spoke with her by phone or she came to visit, I would be wondering if it had already happened. Ironically, it had the opposite effect — it killed me *not* knowing.

When that relationship ended, I learned a lot about this issue, principles, and the meaning of infidelity in this context. First, I learned that not every woman feels a burning desire to be physically intimate to the point of sleeping with another man while hers is in prison. Not every woman uses the rationale that she's "only human" to justify such an act. Secondly, I have come to believe that being in prison doesn't necessitate that I forsake my principles to keep a woman. This is clearly something I wouldn't tolerate if I were *not* in prison — so why tolerate it now? I didn't lose my self-worth, dignity, and my right to be respected by the woman I'm with just because I came to prison. I regretted even relegating myself to that of a desperate man trying to keep his woman by agreeing to let her sleep with other men until I came home. But doing so served as a learning mechanism; it showed me how far we are willing to go in compromising our principles to meet our core needs when faced with severely distressing situations. It's a known fact that when humans experience acute, immense crises, they will desperately cling to those who can offer them comfort, even to the point of compromising their core values and principles.

In no way am I attempting to persuade everyone in a relationship with someone in prison to agree with me on this. I know this is a sensitive, maybe even polarizing, topic that divides people into opposite sides of this argument. What I am saying is that, for me anyway, believing I would be able to cope with it better by not hearing about it was totally untrue. I imagine I'm not alone in this regard.

Furthermore, I firmly believe that a relationship will only thrive when there are sacrifices made by both parties, regardless of the situation, and fidelity and loyalty are preserved. If this is too much to ask, then I submit it may be better to sever the relationship and spare the inevitable agony that will surely be felt by at least one of the parties involved. If not, resentments will build and turmoil will ensue — trust me! Not knowing sounds doable and perhaps even reasonable but will likely end up causing more damage than good in the long run, so why even go there?

IT'S ALL ABOUT TIMING

Anyone in a relationship with someone incarcerated knows how critical it is to be available to answer the phone during certain times of the day. I've found it remarkable how those who love and support us have been willing and able to, day after day, modify their schedules to align with the times we can call.

In my own relationship, my fiancée has answered the phone numerous times while out of breath because she just sprinted across the room to answer the phone in time. Her urgency to answer the phone before it quit ringing is due to her knowing if she is unable to answer, then it's uncertain when I may be able to call back (inmates cannot receive calls). To most people it wouldn't necessarily be a big deal if they were not able to get to the phone in time to answer when their significant other is calling — they would simply call them back. Obviously, she does not have this option. In this circumstance, it is access to the phone that primarily sustains our relationship. Phone calls are crucial to our strength and sense of togetherness. It is the conduit through which we can verbally express our affection for one another. Without this essential luxury, I am not sure we would have made it all these years.

My heart warms over every time I hear her say how she periodically glances at the clock throughout the day, anticipating the precise time she can expect my call. As busy as this career and family-oriented woman is, she still manages to carve out and prioritize time for us to talk. I find this extraordinarily sacrificial, selfless, and admirable. It is humbling for me to know she thinks that much of me to go to great lengths so we can talk regularly.

Just as she is patiently, yet eagerly, awaiting designated times during the day I can call her, I am just as eager to talk to her at those specific times. I do my very best to call at the predetermined times, but contrary to what many people may believe, prisoners also have busy schedules to manage and are not automatically available to do whatever we please. Because I know she is expecting me to call at certain times, if I know ahead of time that I'm not going to be able to do so, I'll leave her an email (yes, fortunately we have that ability) to let her know that I am obligated to do something else at that time and assure her we will talk the next day. Extending this courtesy, I've learned, can go a long way when in this type of relationship because, again, everything is on a schedule and our personal lives are largely affected by these constraints.

I'll admit, a part of me feels somewhat guilty for subjecting such an amazing woman to the burdens of my situation. I know she doesn't deserve to "pay" for what I've done by having to assimilate to the abnormalities of my situation, but she has assured me that although she doesn't like being subjected to the harsh realities of this situation, it is worth it for the relationship we have cultivated and the future we both look forward to. When she puts it that way, I can't agree with her more.

True enough, because prison is an institution that is governed by strict time parameters and limitations on everything we do, our relationships will feel the effects of this. But when two people can accept this fact and find a workable schedule to connect during designated times, it becomes a true testament to their strength and resolve as a couple. Once you've got the timing down, the rest seems to simply fall in place.

DEAR JOHN

Dear John,

I didn't know how I was going to start this letter. I'm not even sure I want to send it, but after doing a lot of thinking last night, I realized there was no 'perfect way' to say what I need to say. So here it goes.

When all of this happened last year and you were taken away from the girls and me, my world crumbled to the ground. I cried for nights, begging God to bring you home, to not allow our family to be broken up any longer. But He must not have heard my plea, John. Why didn't He bring you home to us?

These kids miss you so much, John, and they are still too young to fully understand what has happened and why Daddy isn't here night after night to tuck them in like you used to. I try my best to explain to them in a child appropriate way, but I don't think I'm doing a good enough job. This is so hard.

My family has noticed a significant difference in my mood and demeanor since the sentencing last month. For the entire year while you were still awaiting trial, I held out hope that we'd be granted a miracle — that this nightmare would end. But it didn't. In fact, it got much worse when the jury found you guilty and the judge gave you ten years! I immediately felt my heart sink into my stomach; it has stayed there ever since. I'm so broken, John. I'm so torn right now.

I have not been okay with this situation for a while now and I've struggled with trying to decide what is best for the girls and me. I know we mean the world to you, John — that's not even a question. But I'd be lying if I said this wasn't taking a toll on us as well. So as hard as this is for me to do,

I've made the decision that I never thought I'd make: John, I must say goodbye.

I never saw this as our future when we got together over six years ago. And if you're wondering, no, I haven't met anyone else so please don't think that is why I'm doing this. But I won't lie to you, John; I'm not going to prevent myself from having a future with someone later down the road if and when the time comes that I'm ready for that. Right now, though, that's the furthest thing from my mind.

The main thing I am thinking about now is how our girls are going to deal with this when they're older and begin to understand it. Dammit, John! Why'd you have to go and do something so stupid and put us through this? We don't deserve this!

Anyway, I've already told your mom of my plans and have made arrangements for her to bring the girls to see you in a couple years when they'll be ready for that. As much as I hate what you've put us through, I wouldn't keep them from you. They love you too much for that. So, I guess this is it for now, John. I hope you understand how difficult this has been for me, but I can't go on living like this. It's been pure hell for me, and I can't continue this way. Take care of yourself, John. I'm going to start doing the same.

Sincerely,

Broken-Hearted

Although this is a fictional example, it exemplifies the heart-wrenching "Dear John" letter that is likely the greatest fear someone in a relationship has when they come to prison. When we come to prison, we do our best to cling to people and pieces of our lives because they provide comfort and a sense of familiar security. They help us through our agonizing days of adjustment to our new surroundings and give us hope for the future. But we also understand the mental and emotional burden placed on our loved ones, and fear, as a result, we may eventually lose them.

Although it's certainly understandable how many men would be devastated to receive this dreaded letter, they have no one to blame but themselves. It is not fair to expect women to endure this tremendously difficult circumstance, especially for those who are now forced to raise the children these men left behind on their own, should they stay in the relationship. If anything, this sobering letter should be a harsh revelation of how much these men sacrificed for the reckless lives they *chose* to live. This rock bottom moment should be what precipitates dramatic change in their thoughts, behavior, and character going forward. When "John" is reading that piercing letter, he has no one to blame but himself.

WHAT DIFFERENCE DOES IT MAKE?

It has been brought to my attention that among women who are in relationships with incarcerated men, there are varying statuses, prejudice, and even belittlement. Apparently, there is a belief among some women who have been with their now-incarcerated partner before his incarceration that they are *better*, or their relationship is more authentic, than someone who happened to meet their partner after he was already incarcerated. And they feel this way simply because they knew him before he got locked up — *really?*

Excuse me if I'm missing something, but is it not true that both types of relationships share a common and critical thread, which is that each requires immense sacrifice and endurance through tremendous hardship? Both types of relationships share limited communication and physical barriers. Considering this, it baffles me how one faction of women within this contingent can separate themselves from others who in fact share their fate. Oh, wait a minute — I *do* know why this happens: it's the need to elevate oneself at someone else's expense. This is an unfortunate, yet pervasive, trait of mankind. No matter where we are in life (socially or economically) or what our circumstance is, many of us will look for a psychological advantage by putting others down to build ourselves up. This is a classic way for those who lack self-esteem to instantly boost how they feel about themselves. Blacks do it to blacks, whites do it to whites, Christians do it to Christians, and the list goes on.

If I am to be fair, I would surmise those on the other side of this argument would say because their relationship has more history and has endured tough circumstances both before and during incarceration, it stands to reason their relationship has a greater chance of succeeding after release. If this is their rationale, however, I'm sorry to say this does not hold up to any real measurable test. Where are the statistics to support this claim?

What I have seen time and again are women who leave their men when they get locked up. What I have also seen routinely are men who meet amazing women *while* locked up and go on to have fruitful, thriving relationships beyond prison. My current relationship began and evolved in this fashion after my then-girlfriend (whom I was with before I was incarcerated) left me a year and a half into my sentence. My fiancée and I have now been together for over twelve years! Our relationship is without question the greatest gift I could have asked for. She tells me it is the greatest blessing that has ever happened to her as well. Is our relationship less meaningful because we met *after* I came to prison?

This reminds me of how women would criticize and ridicule other women who joined online dating services; now it's a culturally acceptable practice and you see television commercials advertising it.

There is no monopoly on what makes a relationship valid, credible, or substantive. Relationships are like the people that make them up: diverse in appearance, dynamics, and circumstances. They are built on trust, healthy communication, companionship, intimacy, compassion, and sacrifice. These are some of the essential cornerstones of a healthy relationship.

Prior to today, my naiveté led me to believe most women in relationships of this kind would naturally band together when they met one another. It would seem they would naturally want to support others who share their unique circumstance. Sadly, I've learned this is not always the case. If two people have fallen in love — regardless of how they met — and built their relationship on the aforementioned essentials, what difference does it make *where* they met?

HE DOESN'T DESERVE YOU

I was using the phone on the yard a couple weeks ago when I heard a man who was two or three phones down from me yelling at the top of his lungs at whomever was on the other end of the phone. Everyone in the vicinity stopped what they were doing and instantly became fixated on this expletive-laden tirade this man was unleashing on the person on the other end. This lasted for about a minute or two, but it seemed like much longer. It ended with him violently slamming the phone onto its hook, cutting his hand in the process, and him furiously stomping away.

As dramatic as this scene obviously was, in prison it is commonplace. I've witnessed similar instances while using the phone in my housing unit and even during the face-to-face visits! There are two things that go through my mind when I witness these unfortunate occurrences: He is extremely selfish for treating someone this way, as though they owe him something! And why is she putting up with it? It's as if he has forgotten that *he* put himself in prison — not *her* or anyone else! It's also evident that he takes her for granted and believes she will never leave him because, after all, I'm quite sure this wasn't the first time he has disrespected her or disregarded her feelings.

I do not pretend to know all the dynamics of people's relationships, and by no means am I an expert in this field. But from a basic human, rational standpoint, I don't believe a woman should ever put up with being perpetually degraded by a "man" like that! It's even more perplexing when he's locked up. I don't say this to insinuate that incarcerated men are less forgivable or less deserving of understanding than someone who is not incarcerated, but men who mistreat women while in prison tend to do so because they believe it is everyone else's responsibility to provide their every need while here. It is not! They do it because they take women for granted, and no matter how hard women try to please these men, it will never be enough.

It appears that these men live in a make-believe world where they are the crown jewel of mankind, the king of the universe, and everyone else ought to be subservient to them. They don't say thank you very often because, well, why should they? After all, they believe, people *ought* to be doing these things for them. I understand that no one is perfect, and we all are subject to regrettable outbursts in an angry moment, but that's not what I'm talking about here. I'm strictly referring to men in prison who mistreat, disrespect, and take their girlfriends or wives for granted on a regular basis. This is indicative of their character and is not excusable as an unfortunate moment.

For many of us it was our self-centered nature that brought us to prison. Once we are here, it becomes our responsibility to recognize our shortcomings, address them, and begin to work toward overcoming them. If we don't, the result will be this: men will berate their women for not sending money "on time" or for not answering the phone every time they call. The result will be him embarrassing her during a visit by scolding her for something she didn't do "soon enough" or for not doing it how he wanted it done. He then might get up and walk out of the visiting room as she cries and pleads for him not to leave — no hug, no kiss, and no goodbye. Yet, despite all that he puts her through, he knows when he calls later that night to apologize (for the hundredth time), she will answer his call; when he asks for another favor, she will do her best to please him. And, sadly, the story continues in this chaotic fashion.

Ever heard of tough love? These are classic cases where it could do some good. And if these men still don't learn to appreciate the women who sacrifice so much for them during this situation, he needs to be left alone to think about what he is doing wrong. Bottom line is this: he doesn't deserve you!

WORTH WAITING FOR

As mentioned in previous blogs, we often use various psychological tactics to counter adversity and cope with difficult circumstances in the best, or easiest, way possible. The ways in which inmates count down the remaining time on their sentence vary drastically from inmate to inmate as well as among their loved ones. But we all know that no matter how it is framed, all of us who are incarcerated (and our families) proceed through every day of this journey with constant thoughts of our eventual release.

This topic arises in my relationship with some regularity, and we tend to speak about it in terms of playing the proverbial waiting game. We understand that while every day is yet another day that we are unable to physically be together, it's also one more day closer to that glorious day of reunion. Even when our conversation veers into the harsh and sobering reality of how much time we must still be away from each other, we usually are able to bring our attention back to the fact that what awaits us at the end of this journey is a fulfilled, enriched life together that we have envisioned for all these years. This seems to encourage and uplift us every time.

Clearly, no one in his or her right mind would elect to fall in love with someone in prison and gladly wait years to physically be together. However, when a fulfilling, enriching, beautiful relationship blossoms and flourishes in spite of the difficulties of this circumstance, isn't it rational to conclude this indeed is something worth waiting for? Critics abound, but suffice it to say one of the primary aspirations we as humans have in this life is to find true love; and given the option to have this coveted connection with someone that requires a waiting period of a few years, I believe many would opt in.

If we honestly reflect on life and the things we have obtained over the years (including material possessions and relationships) but no longer possess, we can find many instances where things that were obtained quickly and easily often did not last long. For me personally, these came in the form of rushed relationships that never lasted longer than six months. This was because I was so enthralled with the novelty of the new relationship that I would never take the time to get to know my girlfriend on a deeper level. We never really moved beyond the "honeymoon" phase, and because we never established a true friendship, by the time the novelty wore off, there was not enough substance there to sustain us.

I have never been of the belief that it's constructive to live your life for someone else, but it is also unrealistic to think you can live your life in a way that your behavior doesn't have a direct impact on those around you. Therefore, we must consider how our decisions will affect others. And we increase people's faith and confidence in us when we behave in ways that are healthy and productive.

As difficult as we all know it can be for the women who are sacrificing so much to wait for our eventual return home, it is the conviction of knowing their sacrifice is worth the wait that carries them through, day after day.

IT'S NOTHING PERSONAL

As humans, we become extremely stimulated with an overwhelming euphoria when we meet someone with whom we share an instant, powerful connection. This intense feeling of "walking on cloud nine" is to be expected during the budding stage of a relationship. Naturally, we want to tell anyone and everyone who will listen how amazing the new person in our life is. Women, especially, are all too eager to share with their closest girlfriends how the incredible man they've started dating has all the qualities she had ever hoped to find in a mate; how he is such a gentleman and has made her feel like the most important girl in the world. She emphatically proclaims he is "the one." Men, on the other hand, may in fact share this enthusiasm and *want* to tell their buddies how great the new woman in their life is but tend to hold back to appear as though they're not easily mesmerized by a woman, as this would surely compromise their "manly" image among friends.

Unfortunately, however, the joy and support most women receive from friends and family after sharing a giddy-filled story of how she met and has gotten to know the man of her dreams is rarely felt by women who are with men in prison. No, not even close.

Women who are in relationships with men in prison have by and large learned it is more beneficial to keep quiet about their relationships when in the company of their friends and family. They do this to avoid being harshly judged and criticized. These women are essentially forced to live in a perpetual state of isolation at the realization that no one seems to understand (or care to understand) their decision to be with a man who is incarcerated or believe that their relationship is just as valid and meaningful as conventional relationships. Because this is their reality, they choose to guard themselves from the inevitable venom and cruelty that come from those who are quick to judge and belittle their relationships. The saddest part of this is that the harshest criticism seems to come directly from family.

I will be the first one to admit that I was *not* okay with the fact that my fiancée felt she had to keep our relationship a secret from her family and friends when we first got together. I couldn't understand why she would let the inconsiderate, callous feelings of others dictate how much and in what manner she would talk about me and our relationship. This, I later realized, was a purely selfish viewpoint on my part because, I reasoned, I am not the one who has to hear people's horrible comments spewed my direction. I don't have to sit there while my relationship is being demeaned by people who feel it is unequal to theirs simply because of where my partner is located. When considering this from her perspective, I quickly regretted insisting that she shouldn't care what others think or say about us; that she should boldly proclaim our love to the world. This was a one-sided way of viewing it. Why would I want her to speak about us to people she and I both know don't support us? Why would I want her to be subjected to the ridicule and torment of those who will *never* understand a relationship of this kind? That's not something I would ever want her to endure.

Today, I don't even think twice about it. I'm thoroughly happy with what we have — period! I know one hundred percent how she feels about me and our relationship. I know I mean the world to her and therefore I don't take it personally that she doesn't feel comfortable telling anyone and everyone in her circle about us. After all, why would I, when I know this would only open her up to people's harsh attacks and blistering criticism? A defining manifestation of love is protecting the person you love. This, in my eyes, is exactly what I'm doing by supporting her decision to not publicly talk about our relationship.

HE'S JUST USING YOU . . . OR IS HE?

Perhaps the most commonly held belief regarding men in prison is we all prey on women who are weak and gullible, to get them to send us money or care packages. Many people believe we are eager to enter relationships for the sole purpose of telling an unsuspecting, vulnerable woman whatever she wants to hear to get her to fall in love and subsequently send us anything we ask for, whenever we ask for it. Now, does this happen? Of course, it does! But do men who are *not* in prison also mislead, manipulate, and use women for their personal gain? The point I'm attempting to make is not all of us who are incarcerated are interested in taking advantage of women for financial gain, just as not all men outside of prison are looking to use women.

In the psychopathology class I recently took, I came across a very interesting statistic. I learned that antisocial personality disorder — which is characterized by lacking empathy, remorse, and a desire to be close to people — is diagnosable in approximately 40% of those who are incarcerated (Beidel, Bulik, & Stanley, 2010). These men have a knack for manipulating people for their own personal gain, particularly using their charm on vulnerable women. Of this 40% of the inmate population who qualify to be diagnosed with antisocial personality disorder, one could surmise that a considerable amount of them would have the opportunity to use women for money at some point during their incarceration; but what about the remaining 60% of inmates? Are they also prone to this form of sociopathy? Are they not capable of entering relationships for the sole purpose of loving another human and being loved in return?

I will not settle this debate here in a five-hundred-word blog post, nor do I intend to; I merely wanted to make the point that most inmates are not inherently driven toward this deplorable behavior, as many people seem to believe. The fact is, yes, there are plenty of men in prison who are solely out to use women under the guise of being in a committed, loving relationship; however, there is also a plethora of men who have come to understand and appreciate what is truly valuable and priceless in this world, and they (we) want to experience and enjoy what a meaningful relationship offers. For many of us, relationships of this kind are novel because prior to prison most of us were too self-centered and self-absorbed to even know how to begin to love another person. Now that we are more mature and blessed with such a remarkable opportunity, we want to appreciate and cherish it by being the men these wonderful women deserve.

When we came to prison, we didn't lose our inherent need for love, companionship, and acceptance, to name a few. Because there are women in the world who happen to see us as human beings and perhaps unintentionally fall in love (because they have these same human needs), this should not automatically be viewed as a fake, one-sided, manipulative relationship on the part of the inmate. Not all of us are in for money or snacks; many of us gain the intrinsic reward of simply being in a mutually loving relationship for the first time.

STILL ROOM TO GROW

Have you ever heard the saying, "The day you stop learning is the day you die?" This simply means as long as we are breathing, we can and should be open to learning and growing from our day-to-day experiences. I have found this to be especially true when it comes to romantic relationships.

I've been in a relationship for many years and I feel as though my fiancée and I know each other as well as two people can. Over the years we have learned each other's likes, dislikes, fears, goals, and everything in between. She has been my motivation for striving to be better in every facet of my life because I know she absolutely deserves the very best version of me I can be.

We talk about everything, share our innermost feelings, concerns, and vulnerabilities because, well, that's what love compels people to do. I have never felt more comfortable with anyone in disclosing the things I have about myself because she has shown me I can one hundred percent trust her. She is my best friend in every sense of the word. One may think from the outside looking in that because our relationship appears to be tightly bound by the essential elements of a healthy, fulfilling relationship that there is not much room for growth; this assumption, however, would be mightily wrong!

The fact is even ten years later we are still learning about each other's idiosyncrasies and preferences regarding issues that don't come up regularly. I believe this is imperative for the continued growth and closeness of any relationship. I am still battling with some of my own baggage that at times causes strife in our relationship. She, however, has been incredibly patient and committed to this relationship by forgiving me and helping me overcome my shortcomings. That's what a partnership is about. I'm learning to be more attentive to her "love language" (what she needs from me to feel most loved) and cognizant of what truly bothers her in certain situations. It is the nuances that matter. It is the attentiveness to details that can make all the difference in the world when it comes to the level of intimacy you share with your partner.

When the rare occasion arises where she and I go through a major rift, we take a moment to step back, gather our thoughts, and reconvene to discuss the disagreement rationally and respectfully, understanding this is conducive to the constructive conflict resolution we both desire. We do this without placing blame, fighting over who's right or wrong, or casting stones that we later wish we could take back. Instead, we proceed from the standpoint of asking ourselves how we can learn from this ordeal and become better in the future. By taking this approach, we each have grown and learned something we can apply to our relationship that makes it that much stronger going forward.

For our union to have remained as strong as it has for all these years, it is indeed a testament to what true love can withstand and overcome; but as strong as we are today, we also know we can always be stronger tomorrow. We can and should continue to be willing and committed to learning more about each other to improve our relationship and understand one another better. No matter how long you've been together, how madly in love you are with your partner, please remember there is *always* room to grow.

THEY'LL NEVER UNDERSTAND

The only women who enter, or stay committed to, relationships with men in prison must be grossly overweight, suffer from extremely poor self-esteem, or are mentally unstable. Clearly, this is an absurd misconception that, unfortunately, many people erroneously believe due to prevailing stereotypes about prison, prisoners, and the women who love them. After all, they'd say, why would a beautiful, intelligent, financially-secure woman who can seemingly attract any man she'd like choose to be with someone in prison?

The first error many people make is allowing stereotypes to permeate their thinking process. These are very rigid mental constructs that have been formed by their own and others' isolated experiences, observed occurrences (again in limited number), or unfounded beliefs that have been passed along by others — usually family or friends. No matter the case, stereotypes are *not* an accurate indicator by which we ought to formulate opinions of others, as people will show you who they are as individuals — not a cookie-cutter specimen of your stereotyped expectation. Unfortunately, many who hold the ignorant notion that every woman who chooses to be in a relationship with a man in prison is of one "type" are allowing their stereotypes to guide their faulty thinking.

Many people fail to realize that we don't choose who we love! It's not as if a woman sets out to fall in love with someone in prison (even *I* would question such a decision or pursuit). Rather, she likely became drawn to him because of his qualities and how he responded to her needs, despite his physical circumstances. They could build their connection and chemistry over time as they engaged in meaningful conversation — just like any other relationship develops.

Those on the outside looking in who are judgmental and critical are choosing to only view it from a position of contempt for the incarcerated individual whom they see as an "inmate" — not a person. They have concluded he is not worthy or deserving of forgiveness, understanding, compassion, or any form of human decency. Therefore, they will never change their opinion until they first begin to see him as a human being who made a costly mistake but can ultimately be redeemed.

My fiancée did not write her initial letter to me with the intent of building a romantic relationship. In fact, she thought that it would *not* happen because she was not remotely interested in that type of correspondence. Her only goal was to "brighten an inmate's day," after she had watched a documentary about prisoners and saw how someone's day can be made so much better by simply receiving a letter from someone from the outside. So, she decided she would write to me after carefully scrutinizing countless inmate pen pal ads online.

We didn't enter into a romantic relationship until after approximately six months later, after having exchanged countless genuine, heartfelt letters and phone calls which enabled us to connect on a deep, intimate level. The point I'm trying to make is she still doesn't feel totally comfortable with broadcasting our relationship to everyone at her job or to her casual friends because of the inherent judgment she would face. This hurt me in years' past because my position was our relationship should supersede anyone's negative opinion about it, but I now understand her feelings. The last thing I'd want is for her to be ridiculed because she's in love with me. She tells me, "People will just never understand, Martin; they'll never give you the benefit of the doubt because of where you are — it's just not fair!" She's right; it's not fair, but it's life. There will always be naysayers, detractors, and outright "haters." But what matters is *she* knows why she's in this relationship and *you* know why you're in yours. You can try to convince them to see it the way you see it, but the fact remains, for the most part, they'll never understand.

ADVANTAGES OF A PRISON RELATIONSHIP

Anyone in a relationship with someone in prison knows it can be extremely difficult at times. It is predicated on the essentials of a true, healthy, meaningful relationship — communication, trust, honesty, and everything in between. When these components are intact, they can be the foundation to a wonderful, thriving, fulfilling union. However, we are all human and, therefore, I would be remiss if I failed to underscore the importance of the physical intimacy that is also an integral part of a relationship. However, contrary to what many people think, this does not just entail the sexual contact (although this seems to be the most felt void by both parties in a prison relationship) but also includes other aspects of intimacy such as holding hands, cuddling at night, sharing a meal together, or merely giving a brief hug and kiss when departing each other's presence.

I've learned in my own relationship that to focus on the things we are incapable of (due to the obvious physical constraints) would only inhibit our ability to highlight and be grateful for all the things we *do* have. If you are in a relationship with someone who is locked up, then you know it is fundamental to accept the physical limitations while simultaneously appreciating the elements that have given you a strong, healthy relationship. Many people in the free world have a tough time understanding how a sane, rational woman can be happy in a relationship of this kind. But the answer is very comprehensible when you think about it: an emotional connection sustains a relationship; sex (and other physical touch) is but *one* expression of that emotional connection.

My relationship has its issues like any other (well, like any other *prison* relationship), but I believe we are also at a great advantage to overcome these difficulties because our foundation has been developed and sustained on the true principles that create a solid bond between two people. I look at my relationship as a unique opportunity for me to grow in the aspects that I have needed to be the man she deserves. This situation has forced me to mature and grow in the areas of selflessness, communication, and sacrifice. For that, I am eternally grateful.

Being in a relationship of this kind has its salient downfalls that are uncharacteristic of a conventional relationship, but, despite these challenges, I believe it has its unique opportunities to develop the vital aspects of a healthy partnership that perhaps others do not. If you are reading this as someone who is happily fulfilled in a relationship of this kind, then you know exactly what I'm talking about.

It appears to me that most relationships that develop outside of prison tend to quickly add sexual intimacy. This is to be expected as we are naturally, physically drawn to someone we care about and, depending on one's personal beliefs, desire to be intimate with them. This is not inherently bad for a relationship, although doing so can cause a couple to become "sidetracked" from getting to know each other on a deeper level. Perhaps the primary advantage of a "prison relationship" is that in the forced absence of each other's physical presence, they are able to focus on the essentials of building a sustainable bond with one another.

SHE'S BETTER THAN I DESERVE

I had been in a two-year relationship when I came to prison over ten years ago. Throughout that entire time, I cheated on her, disregarded her feelings, and lived as though she should consider my wants and needs before her own — if she were to consider hers at all! I had never learned to love a woman because I had never learned how to love myself. I took her love for granted and selfishly expected her to stay committed to me throughout my entire seventeen-year sentence — despite how I had mistreated her! Not surprisingly, she left me about a year and a half into my incarceration. I was devastated and struggled to get over my self-pity when this happened. Despite the fact I knew I deserved it, part of me, irrationally, felt like the victim. *How dare she leave me when I need her the most,* I thought. Eventually, however, I matured, took an honest look at my shortcomings and began to work on them; I understood if I was ever going to be worthy of a good woman's love and commitment, I'd better first be a quality man who can reciprocate love and devotion.

To mitigate my loneliness, I joined a pen pal website and shortly thereafter met an amazing woman. Initially, we were content with strictly being friends and writing each other without any expectations of anything more intimate. However, over the next several months of getting to know one another, our attraction to each other grew and we established a romantic relationship.

She has been my best friend, confidant, rock and biggest supporter throughout this very arduous time. She is everything I could ask for in a woman and life partner. We know each other like the backs of our hands and focus on appreciating what we *do* have while not dwelling on what we *don't*. This tends to help us through the periods of difficulty when the burden of this situation especially weighs heavily on her. Granted, our relationship is not perfect and has had many trying times (like any relationship), but we always find our way back to the unwavering belief that we are more compatible with each other than we have been in prior relationships; that our foundation is stronger than the difficulties of this situation. I did absolutely nothing to deserve this angel of a woman who walked into my life, sacrificed more than any person should ever have to, and believed in me enough to help me pursue all my goals and dreams. Yet, here she is.

I tell her how much I appreciate her as often as I can so she will never doubt it. I tell her how she continually inspires me to be a better man so she will know the impact she has in my life. I tell her how no other woman can fulfill me the way she does so she'll know how truly unique and cherished she is. Yet, I know in my heart of hearts that despite all of this, she is still better than I deserve.

LOVE IS . . .

Love is . . . well, the definitions include an endless list of adjectives that all ring true when describing this abstract noun. Then again, many would argue that love is an action word, otherwise known as a verb. We all can agree that love *does*. It is felt, not just heard. It is evident, not just implied. With Valentine's Day on the horizon — the ultimate day of celebration of love — I wanted to discuss the extraordinary love that manifests in the lives of countless inmates across this vast country by family and friends.

Without attempting to provide an exhaustive list of definitions of what I personally believe love is, I would like to assert what I know love to include. Love is commitment. Love is sacrificial. Love is enduring and stubborn. It is bold and yet compassionate at the same time. Love is steady and diligent and selfless. Love can both heal and hurt. Love has the unique power to lift us, carry us, and place us on a sturdy platform above the chaos that exists all around us. Indeed, this is exactly what I see in the parents, girlfriends, wives, siblings, children, and grandparents who support their incarcerated loved ones month after month, year after year.

I'm always in awe when I enter the visiting room and see people of all ages there to visit their confined loved ones. After visiting concludes, I head back to my cell feeling emotionally energized and humbled that my family would continually make the long trip to see me. I can't help but also think about the many miles all those visitors had to see their loved ones for only a couple hours, the time they may have had to take off work, the money spent for gas, food, hotel rooms, and the planning that went into making the visit possible. I'm compelled to think about the enormous sacrifice they make to keep money on phone accounts so their son or daughter, brother or sister, husband or wife, girlfriend or boyfriend can call home and feel loved; or the money they provide for commissary that will perhaps make their time a bit more comfortable.

Many people in society often criticize women for sticking by their men in prison, but what they fail to realize is that love is tenacious. It is not bound by physical circumstance or weakened by peer pressure — so they're wasting their breath! What I find most tragic, however, is the judgment and shame families face when their son or daughter is in this dreaded situation. Yet, love will not be intimidated or reduced to silence! Love rises to the occasion time and again. It has stood the test of time and conquered the most trying battles humans have faced throughout mankind's existence.

I understand that remaining loyal to your incarcerated loved ones is no easy task. I'd imagine many of you feel mentally, emotionally, and physically exhausted at times as you have spent sleepless nights worrying about your loved ones in such a hostile dwelling, or simply missing them more than you thought was humanly possible on birthdays and other important holidays. But what I want to encourage you to do in these moments of vulnerability is to take a minute to acknowledge the power of love — the same love that has carried you thus far; the same love that keeps your incarcerated loved one strong and optimistic day in and day out. Understand you are human and will have overwhelming moments of pain and weakness that will inevitably soak your pillow — and that's perfectly okay. In fact, it's therapeutic! That's another thing that love does — it makes you feel.

Although this Valentine's Day may not be spent ideally with your loved one, please take solace in knowing what you're exhibiting daily is *exactly* what this holiday is all about — love. We on the inside could not be as optimistic, grounded, resilient, and determined to overcome our circumstance if it were not for your unwavering love and support. Thank you to all who make tremendous sacrifices on a routine basis to show your love and make your incarcerated loved one's time in prison much more manageable. You are all angels, and this is without question *your* day! We acknowledge you, celebrate you, and love you! Happy Valentine's Day.

PART IV

The Ripple Effect

A PEBBLE IN THE POND

As children, during our summer vacation from school, my friends and I would go to the park and eagerly seek out a pond to play one of our favorite games. After arriving at the pond, we would enthusiastically search for the perfect-sized pebbles that we could skip across the water with a twist of our arm and flick of our wrist. The object, as many of you know, was to skip them across the pond as far as we could get them to go. Some rocks would effortlessly hop across the still water as if they had life of their own, while others would simply hit the water with a thud and instantly sink to the bottom. We never got bored with this activity as we vigorously competed with one another for the "farthest-rock-skipping" award.

Another fascinating aspect of this activity was the ripple effect each pebble invariably created the instant it made violent contact with the pond. We would all marvel at the rapid spread of circular waves that extended outward from the center of the small pebble that forcefully met the calm water. It amazed me how a single pebble, so small and seemingly harmless, could cause such a massive impact on the vast body of water surrounding it.

I now sit here in a prison cell and reflect on these fond childhood memories, but the warm nostalgia of innocent child's play is not what seizes my attention in those moments. I now view the ripple effect of those pebbles representing the enormous hurt I have inflicted on many people by my actions. As I lived my life prior to prison while drinking daily, cheating on my girlfriend, recklessly partying every weekend, and driving intoxicated on a regular basis, I never even stopped to consider how my careless actions could affect those who love me and many others.

My family does not deserve to be subjected to dehumanizing institutional rules when they come to visit me. My nieces and nephew should not have to grow up only seeing their uncle a few times a year and not having me present for their birthdays, Christmases, and graduations. My fiancée does not deserve having to look at other couples with envy as they enjoy the simple presence of each other's company because I chose to live recklessly and put myself here for over seventeen years. I have no choice but to come to terms with and understand the profound impact that my selfish actions have had on countless people in my life. Obviously, my intent was never to hurt those I love the most in this world; but if I'm to be brutally honest in this analysis, that's *exactly* the choice I made when I lived a life that disregarded them and their feelings. It's selfish and unrealistic to think that our actions don't affect others, but this is the way I chose to live. I assumed I would be the only one who would have to live with the consequences of my actions — boy, was I wrong!

I've come to understand what is required of you when you claim to love someone. I profess to love my fiancée, family, extended family, and friends, so I must conduct myself in a way that reflects that proclamation. Had I understood the ripple effect concept years earlier, who knows what the trajectory of my life would have been. Having said this, I am not one to live in the past. It does me no good to dwell on the past and what could have been, but what I *will* do going forward is remain cognizant that I am a part of a network of people, a group of loved ones that I affect and am affected by. This interdependent bond — a small community if you will — collectively rises and falls with the actions and outcomes of its members' behavior. Knowing this then, I am committed to doing my part by being an asset to the group, not someone who becomes an impediment to it. I vow to not be the pebble responsible for the devastation sent out by the reverberating ripple caused by my actions.

THE POWER OF A LETTER

Adjusting to prison is no easy feat. I liken it to being blindfolded, put on an airplane, and taken to a remote location somewhere on this vast earth and dropped off in a foreign land with no resources. You are left with nothing but your own wits and ability to adapt to and navigate your new circumstances as best you can. I make this adaptation process sound easy, but I assure you that for many of us in prison, it is the most stressful, arduous time we will endure. Furthermore, we all possess very different coping abilities and mechanisms to get through these tough times.

Considering this, it's no wonder that we tend to fare much better when we have support from those who sacrifice a great deal to support us in any way they can. But there are many loved ones of those who are incarcerated who don't necessarily know how they can best help their loved ones. Should they write letters often? Send money? Order magazine subscriptions? Visit? I don't pretend to know what every inmate needs to best get through their time, but having been incarcerated for nearly twelve years now, I can say I've never heard anyone complain about getting "too much" mail/pictures from their loved ones. In my opinion, this appears to be the consensus number one expression of support for someone who is locked up. I know life is very busy for many of you (especially those of you with children), and any rationally-minded individual should understand why you wouldn't have time to write regularly, but mail appears to have an intrinsic value that cannot be obtained any other way.

A letter is invaluable because we can, at any time, re-read it as a source of comfort during many lonely nights. I cannot count how many times I have gained strength by reading old letters from loved ones after difficult days when I felt like this nightmare would never end. I have kept sentimental cards that always lift my spirits and encourage me when I'm having a difficult day and need a pick-me-up.

In speaking with other inmates, many have expressed how ecstatic they would be to receive "two written lines" on a piece of paper from an old friend or family member they haven't heard from in years. In other words, it wouldn't take a lengthy letter to make him or her feel loved — even a brief note would be deeply appreciated. It is less about the length of a letter than the thought. We know it takes a lot for you to set aside other things to sit down, write a letter, and send it out in the mail the old-fashioned way.

You need not overthink what the "best" way to provide support to your incarcerated loved one is because I can assure you that showing your presence in their life in any way you can will be greatly appreciated. It just seems to me that the letters and cards we receive carry an unmatched value in this situation, especially when we are locked down at night and left with nothing but our wandering thoughts and the stark reality of our situation.

LET THEM LOVE YOU

Many would say it is paradoxical that someone in prison would long to have the support of their loved ones, yet be reluctant and even deny these very people the opportunity to show their love and support by doing things for them during this most challenging time. To be clearer, many prisoners will outright refuse to ask for and/or accept money, books, magazine subscriptions, care packages, or anything else that their loved ones offer to do for them to make their prison stay more comfortable. But why? Why would someone in this horrid circumstance deny luxuries made available by people who love them and merely want to help?

For many men, part of our identity is rooted in independence and industry. Our culture socializes us to embrace the notion that we are only a "real man" if we can provide life's necessities for our families and ourselves. We are not to ask anyone for anything, lest we be deemed incompetent and pitiful — a poor excuse for a man.

This premise, however, runs counter to the necessity of relying on others when we come to prison. Because we are obviously in a deprived state and would therefore greatly benefit from the support offered by those on the outside who love us, we are almost forced into a dependent role should we accept their help. For those who are especially self-reliant and proud, they struggle with accepting this much-needed help for fear of taking a hit to their self-esteem and identity as a man. This stance is not only counterproductive for the inmate in need, it also has a severe consequence for the loved ones looking to do the limited things they can to show their love and support.

People express love in many ways. Some people prefer to spend quality time, while others enjoy surprising their significant others with gifts when they arrive home. Some will use physical touch to show their affection while others prefer to do random acts of kindness and service for their partner. Unquestionably, we all, during our relationships, display all of these affectionate behaviors; it just so happens that we innately lean more toward one of these expressions of love over the others.

When we come to prison, people who love us are then compelled, in a sense, to show their love and affection in very limited ways. Family members, wives, girlfriends, and others strive to do whatever they can to show their unwavering support. Their need to express their immense love for us feels like it has been strangled and stifled by the inherent constraints imposed by prison, leaving them feeling like their help is still insufficient. Accepting this to be true, why would we then put our pride over their ability and desire to show their love for us? How selfish! How selfish it is to prohibit those who love us to express their love the only way they can during this extremely difficult situation (for us and them). Admittedly, I also have struggled at times to accept gestures of support from people who want to help me; but the more I contemplate it and take to heart the words I'm writing now, the more I soften my stubborn stance and allow them to love me the only way they can under these circumstances.

THE AGONY OF A VISIT

No doubt, the highlight of any inmate's day, week, or month is when their name is called for a visit. This is the time we get to finally have physical contact with the people who mean the most to us. A brief hug and kiss can be enough to savor a moment of comfort for an entire month. It is a time of jubilant conversation and unbridled joy that, for moments throughout, can allow us to momentarily "forget" we are not free to go when the visiting session ends abruptly. Ah, yes, the coveted visit. But what about when it *is* time to say goodbye and our families, friends, and other loved ones are forced to leave us behind? What is the impact of this part of the experience? Please allow me to explain.

I recently had a great visit with my twin brother, older sister, twelve-year-old niece, and eighteen-year-old nephew. We caught up on many things, including what all my friends had been doing in their lives, what some of my extended family members had been up to, and discussed other somewhat trivial matters. We shared popcorn, drank soda, took pictures, and all in all enjoyed our three-hour afternoon visit. When the visit ended, I hugged and thanked them for coming. I then sat down in my seat and patiently waited for the remaining visitors to line up along the wall to be escorted out by the correctional officer.

To my right (about five feet away) I noticed a small boy clutching his dad's leg. The inmate hugged his son with affection and told him, "Daddy loves you, Son. You have to go with Grandma so you guys can go home now, 'k?" The child reluctantly released his dad's leg and childishly skipped to his caregiver. As the line of visitors began to file out of the room, we all waved one last time to our loved ones; the little boy was looking over his shoulder and vigorously waving to his confined father. Then, in a sudden flash, the boy darted from the line of people back to his daddy. He clutched the man's leg seemingly tighter than the first time. The father again comforted his toddler as best he could, and I could see the anguish was just as deep for him as it was for the child. The correctional officers, surprisingly, did not intervene to hurry the kid along, knowing (I'm assuming) this was but a few seconds to them but meant so much more to this confined father and his innocent son. After several seconds, the boy again reluctantly returned to his grandparent for good.

 I went back to my cell that afternoon feeling a gamut of emotions. I not only contemplated missing my own family in the immediate aftermath of their departure and not knowing when I'd see them again, but I also couldn't help but imagine the agony that man and his young child must have felt for hours or days after their emotional visit. The mental and emotional adjustment I have been forced to make after returning to my cell after many visits have physically depleted me on numerous occasions. It is no easy transition to say the least. Sure, visits are greatly appreciated and I'm very thankful every time I get one, but the agony that ensues in the aftermath, well, that part I could live without.

DISCONNECTED

I recently wrote a blog post about how difficult it can be for some inmates to accept help from their loved ones who want to support them through this arduous time. I wrote about the selfishness that is exhibited by the inmate who prevents their loved ones from helping them because they are stubborn, proud, and independent to a fault. I will now use this blog to further explain the mentality behind this and why some inmates choose this approach.

When we come to prison, many of us desperately hope that those we have considered friends for many years would remain in contact with us by writing letters, accepting our phone calls, and coming to visit us. We tend to cling more tightly to our romantic partners with the hope they will stay by our side and provide the comfort, security, and reassurance that we deeply desire. We hope (or even expect) our family members will visit us often, put money on our commissary accounts, and continually show their care and concern for our well-being. These are things we hope those in our lives will do to show their devotion and affirm their love and commitment to us during our time of need. Without discussing the reasonability of these expectations, I think we can all agree this is a normal response when someone is facing the most challenging circumstance of their life. But what if I told you there are a great number of prisoners who *choose* to disconnect themselves from all contact with people on the outside, even people who *want* to be there for them?

I was shocked to learn that these people exist. I was even more astonished to learn there were so many here who are of this mindset! In meeting and speaking with them over time, I learned that all their reasons for rejecting the help that has been offered by friends and family were very similar, if not virtually the same. What they told me was they have decided to cut off all contact with their families, friends, wives and girlfriends in order to psychologically cope with this ordeal. Many of them were (and are) serving over ten years and felt it would be too emotionally difficult for them to hold on to their closest relationships, primarily because they accepted the fact they couldn't maintain those relationships in the way they had prior to coming to prison. They assume it's easier to mentally block these people out of their lives rather than embrace them and worry about what was happening to them and what they were doing, knowing they couldn't help or protect them.

Through my studies in psychology, I've learned that some people tend to mentally isolate themselves from emotionally challenging circumstances as a defense mechanism; but to witness this firsthand from men who are in this situation and whom I thought would gladly welcome support from people who offered it was nothing short of remarkable. These men appeared to be totally at peace with their conscious decision to isolate, even all these years later, with no regrets.

Naturally, many (if not all) of you and others in the free world would immediately conclude this is a selfish, inconsiderate act on the part of the inmate. He/she isn't even thinking about how this affects their families, friends, and loved ones. I can certainly appreciate this view, but when humans are faced with extreme distress, many will employ defense mechanisms just as extreme to help counter their anguish. Therefore, I want to caution anyone out there who is witnessing this behavior in their incarcerated loved one to not take it personally (easier said than done, I know), assure them you can appreciate why they would want to isolate (albeit you may disagree), but that you are nonetheless there for them to help them get through the situation, not make it more difficult. This means you might not insist on visiting every other weekend, writing every week, or asking them to call you often. These things can cause a mental strain for them because they may become overly concerned with "outside" affairs that they have no control over. As difficult as this may be for you, it may be what they need for their peace of mind. We all deal with adversity differently, and for some this comes in the form of voluntary disconnection.

MOM, IT'S NOT YOUR FAULT

In my heart of hearts, I believe most mothers raise their children the very best they can, instilling in them the morals and values most people in society uphold. Mothers have a natural instinct to sacrifice whatever they can for the welfare of their children. Unfortunately, many women are left to raise their children without the help of the man (or men) who fathered their children; yet many still do a remarkable job at providing for their children the necessities to sustain life and the teachings that only a responsible parent can give. Their tenacity and spirit are more than impressive and commendable.

I didn't realize the pain I had caused my mother when I landed myself in prison at the ripe old age of nineteen until she came to visit me in prison for the first time. The grief was written all over her face and in her somber tone. Her sorrow and sense of culpability for where I had ended up was made evident during our conversation when she futilely searched for ways she could have "done better" to prevent my circumstance from happening. At the time, I didn't understand the concept of personal responsibility, so in my narrow-minded perspective it was not only her fault but also my friends' who participated in the crime with me, society at large, and anyone else I could deflect the blame onto.

Today, as a more mature, wise man, I take a profoundly distinct perspective on life and the notion of responsibility. I know without question that my wonderful and loving mom did the absolute best she could in raising my siblings and me. She loved us, spent quality time with us, instilled wholesome values in us, nurtured us, and taught us everything she knew would be beneficial to know in this life. I came to understand that it was my *own* choices as a teen in search of independence that led me astray from my childhood teachings and pursue a life of self-destruction that would land me in prison for many years. After all, my sisters and twin brother have only seen the inside of a jail or prison when they've come to visit me. This, in my estimation, is evidence that it was not my Mom's lack of parental ability but my own reckless choices that led to my downfall — period!

Parents naturally look inward and search for explanations as to why their child has gone astray and ended up in prison. They know, as parents, they are charged with raising their kids to do the right things when no one is watching and grow up to become honest, hard-working people; and when this doesn't happen, they tend to unfairly blame themselves. I am not altogether making the assertion that this is an unhealthy practice, but it certainly *can* be when it is taken to the extreme. In my estimation, when this is applied to the case of an adult child who has gone to prison because of having strayed (for whatever reasons) from their parents' upbringing, the parent(s) should not look within to explain this outcome. In other words, you can't take responsibility for *everything* your children do that don't align with the principles you instilled (or tried to) in them. Often when young people decide to engage in behavior that puts them on a path to prison, it's not because the parents did something irreversibly wrong in raising them; rather, it is because the child felt they were invincible and acted on impulse or relied on a faulty rationale to justify their problematic behavior. Regardless of how these kids (or adults) justify their behavior, one thing is for sure: it is not automatically Mom's fault!

A MEAL I WON'T FORGET

Typically, meals served in prison are anything but memorable — unless it's because it's the worst food you've ever tasted. They are, for the most part, not only forgettable but also regrettable! Yesterday, however, I cannot say this was the case. In fact, the meal I ate yesterday was anything but the standard unappetizing meal we are presented with on a daily basis. No, this one was both appealing to my taste buds and, more importantly, heartwarming to my soul. I'd be glad to explain.

The visiting room began to fill with visitors at an unusual time of 5:30 pm (normally visiting ends at 3:45 pm). Many were guests of inmates — friends, family, significant others — while others were community members who had been invited for their participation in many of the fundraisers they'd helped coordinate between the prison and organizations. By the time 6:00 pm rolled around, there were anywhere between one-hundred-thirty and one-hundred-fifty people in attendance! For the most part, people stood or sat and mingled very casually with their guests until the event got underway.

Among the many guests was my twin brother. I invited him to join me for this annual dinner that is hosted by the inmate Weusi Umoja cultural club (of which I am now secretary). I would have liked to invite more of my family but, due to limited space, we are only allowed to have one guest to dine with. We sat, talked, listened to music, and socialized with other inmates and their guests as we waited for the club's president to address the crowd and invite us to get in line for the food.

While standing in line to be served (the food was purchased at a local grocery store and prepared in the prison kitchen), my brother and I discussed the significance of the occasion, not in the context of it being the club's annual banquet, but from a more personal sentiment. He expressed to me that as he was driving here it dawned on him that this would be the first meal in over ten years that we would have together. We both paused for a moment to let that reality sink in, to appreciate that we were now able to relish this rare and monumental gift.

We piled our plates with baby-back ribs, barbecue chicken tenderloins, barbecue pork loin, crab salad, jambalaya, fresh vegetables and fruit, sweet corn bread, and later returned for "Mississippi mud pie" and ice cream. We sat, ate, and took pictures to capture the preciousness of our moments. Around the room others created their own cherished memories. Many took pictures with friends, visitors, and their significant others. This was the only time we would be allowed to freely take pictures in a setting like this, so we all took advantage of the rare opportunity.

As the social event neared its conclusion (around 8:00 pm) I couldn't help but become overwhelmed with gratitude for the special time that I was able to spend with my brother. I told him, "Man, it was so nice to spend our first evening together in over ten years!" He replied, "Yeah, I guess this *was* our first evening together, huh?" Moments later the music wound down and a voice came over the intercom directing everyone to say their goodbyes. I hugged my brother, reiterated my sincere gratitude for him sharing a meal with me, and wished him a safe trip home.

As I headed back to my housing unit, I was overjoyed with what had just transpired. It was such a refreshing, "non-prison" moment that I would never forget. The food was a special treat in and of itself, but my true satiation came from merely being able to sit and enjoy a nice meal with my brother. Indeed, this was a meal I'll never forget.

THE TIME IS NEVER ENOUGH

I anxiously paced my cell in eager anticipation of my name being called over the muffled unit's intercom system. I knew my family would arrive on time — they always do. But since this would be my first visit since arriving at this prison, I accepted the possibility that they might have some trouble finding it — hopefully not, though. Then it came. At 1:31 pm the officer popped my cell door and announced I had a visit. Nervous and excited, I made my way down the long corridor, past the central control station where the officer verified my identity and proceeded to the visiting area.

Upon entrance into the visiting room, I handed the sergeant my ID card and proceeded into the large, air-conditioned, well-lit room that was filled with women, children, and other loved ones. I immediately spotted my brother, sister, niece, and a good friend whom I've known for nearly twenty years. I greeted them all with a hug, thanked them for coming, and we took our seats to begin discussing how I have managed to adjust to this new prison. We also discussed what has changed in their world and anything else we felt was relevant to talk about.

Moments later I was surprised and excited to learn I could accompany my brother to the vending machine to point out to him what I wanted to snack on, as this had been prohibited at my former prison. Merely standing there with him while he asked me what I wanted was a remarkable moment in and of itself — a moment of normality if you will. After retrieving our chips, candy, and drinks, we headed back to our chairs where we seamlessly joined the conversation that was already in session among my other visitors. We laughed at times, were serious at other times, and never found ourselves at an awkward moment of silence that I think we all subconsciously hope doesn't happen during one of these precious visits.

A short time later, while in mid-sentence, I noticed everyone around us began to stand up almost in unison to say goodbye to their loved ones. I couldn't believe it was 3:45 already! It seemed like we were just getting started — now it was over! I still had so much to say, so much to hear from them, and so much — well, it doesn't matter now. The sergeant stood in the middle of the room and announced loud enough to abruptly interrupt everyone in mid-sentence, "Visiting is now over! Visitors, say a brief goodbye and head for the door." I affectionately hugged each one of them just as we had at the beginning of our meeting. And just like that, they were gone. It was over. I wouldn't know how long it would be before I would see them again. They were escorted back to freedom; I was directed back to confinement.

I have savored that two-hour-fifteen-minute visit all night, and as I write this I'm still comforted by this sentimental retrospection.

I know I am fortunate and blessed to have family and friends who come visit me because, sadly, I see countless men here who have *never* had a visit. I do not take my loved ones' commitment to coming to see me for granted. But even though I'm extremely grateful for the opportunity to spend quality time with them, the time spent just never seems to be enough.

AN OASIS IN A BARBED-WIRE DESERT

I set my alarm clock for 5:45 a.m. so I could wake up early enough to sign up for a haircut this morning. I peeled myself out of bed, brushed my teeth, washed my face, and headed to the chow hall. I ate fried eggs, toast, hash browns, and bacon; then I came back to my cell to wait to be called for my haircut.

Two hours later the officer called my name and popped my cell door. A friend of mine works in the barbershop so I sat in his chair, as I was one of the first ones to arrive for a haircut that morning. I told him to take his time, as I wanted to look my best later that afternoon. He did a great job. I thanked him and returned to my unit to shower.

The afternoon arrived and I became more anxious. I took my pressed jeans and dark blue T-shirt from underneath my mattress where they had been since the last time that I wore them to a visit. I put them on, brushed my hair, lathered lotion on my upper body, and began to pace my space in eager anticipation. I must have walked a mile in my six-by-nine cell for the next forty-five minutes until my name was called over the unit's PA system: "Lockett, you have a visit."

I speed-walked in excitement down the long corridor to the visiting area that held my loved ones — the people who have been in my corner since this nightmare began over ten years ago. They all stood as I entered the room; we embraced, sat down and talked, laughed, and enjoyed each other's company. During our visit, as I always do, I scanned the room to see other inmates enjoying the company of their visitors as well. Little kids scurried about, oblivious to the nature and magnitude of their surroundings. Women held their men tightly and passionately kissed them at the beginning and end of their visit. Visiting parents and grandparents affectionately embraced their confined kids and grandkids.

It goes without saying that visits are easily the highlight of any inmate's day, week, month, and even year! It is during these very human moments that we almost "forget" where we are, as though we are back in our home environment for a brief period. Well, perhaps I've gone a little too far with this illustration, but you understand my point.

It personally encourages and touches me in a remarkable way when I'm in the visiting room — like today — and I see dozens of people there to see their incarcerated loved ones. As many of you know, there are so many more who *don't* get visits in this situation than do. Contact with friends and family in this circumstance, I believe, is critical to our mental vitality and sense of morale; it gives us a reason to hope, believe, and aspire to have a greater life after prison, knowing we have a support system we can rely on to help us achieve our goals. It's refreshing to see that families haven't given up on their condemned loved ones, to see they still support them through their darkest hour.

I took pictures with my family and ate candy, chips, and cookies from the vending machine. We discussed my goals that I've been diligently and vigorously working toward, and I explained to them exactly how these milestones will translate to a promising career when I get out. They caught me up on the lives of my extended family and some of my childhood friends. It was just a good ole' wholesome time with those I love the most in this world. I imagine everyone else in that room did the same and shared the same or similar appreciation for having the company of their visitor(s).

Like always, it's emotionally painful to see them leave, to watch them return to freedom without me while I return to a cell. But I would not trade the solace that my visits provide me during this very difficult time for anything. They are my mental release, my oasis in the middle of a barbed-wire desert.

ALL ABOUT THE KIDS

As a member of the Weusi Umoja African American club here at the prison, today I had the honor and privilege of participating and helping in this year's annual backpack giveaway.

Apparently, I learned, every year the club solicits and receives grants from local businesses to purchase backpacks for kids of inmates ranging from kindergarten through twelfth grade. Stored inside these various backpacks is an abundance of supplies such as paper, pencils/pens, binders, folders, note cards, rulers, and other items kids use to learn.

When I arrived in the visiting room this afternoon, I took a seat behind the small table where an assortment of these backpacks was being displayed for kids of all ages. Younger kids could pick from many vinyl bright-colored backpacks, while older kids could choose one of the canvas-based, dark-colored ones. There was something for everyone.

It wasn't long before the first kid showed up to our table with his dad (an inmate) and mom to peruse the display of backpacks. The young boy spotted one that drew his interest and then looked to his dad for approval. Dad approved and the child turned his attention to us, pointing out the backpack he wanted. We happily told him to take it. He cheerfully opened it up to find the multitude of supplies he could use. His dad did not let him walk away without saying thank you; we told him he was most welcome and could show us how thankful he was by doing his very best in school this upcoming school year.

Over the next couple hours many parents showed up — taking a moment from their visits — to get backpacks for their kids, and we were glad to accommodate them. They expressed how grateful they were and how much this meant to them as many didn't know how they were going to be able to afford all the supplies they needed for the school year that was right around the corner. Personally, it was very gratifying to hear how appreciative they were for what we *inmates* were able to provide them. It's not often we are on the right side of the give-take dynamic. At one point or another, most inmates have taken things from people they know and love, from society and employers, leaving matters worse off than before they showed up. Today, however, it felt great to be on the other end of that exchange.

Before the day wrapped up, my heart was extraordinarily touched when three children we had given backpacks to earlier approached our table to present us with drawings they had gone back to their visiting area to create. On these drawings were childlike crayon messages of thanks for the backpacks they received. They handed their masterpieces to us with big smiles on their little faces, again verbally thanking us for what we'd done. The three of us working that day humbly accepted their drawings, thanked them for their incredible gesture, and taped them to the front of the desk so all could see the beautiful art they'd made.

The two and a half hours spent today handing out backpacks to families who needed them more than most, and knowing how appreciative the parents were, gave me one of the greatest feelings I've experienced in my nearly eleven years of incarceration. There is no greater feeling than knowing you are bringing a smile to kids' faces and bringing much needed relief to parents who undoubtedly struggle to provide their children with everything they need, especially considering that one-half of the earning power for their family is in prison. Coming from an environment where we inmates sometimes hold ourselves as the center of attention and believe our needs are more important than anyone else's, it was refreshing to see the attention was focused on where it needed to be today. Indeed, today was all about the kids.

WHERE HAS THE TIME GONE?

Along with the summer weather comes longer days, outside barbecues, high school proms and graduations. I remember these days from my high school years but having been removed from that for nearly twenty years now, I usually must consciously think about these momentous rites of passage taking place all over the country. Furthermore, being incarcerated has kept me out of touch with these customary events even more so than normal. But this year is different.

This year (in fact in approximately two weeks) my nephew will be graduating from high school and my niece will be graduating with a bachelor's degree from Portland State University. Why am I highlighting this? Besides the obvious fact that I'm an extremely proud uncle, these occasions have also forced me to put into perspective just how much time has gone by in my absence and all the things I've missed.

I have found it useful to count my years in seasons. When the softball equipment is brought out, I know it's summertime. When evening access to the yard ends, I know it is fall. Before I know it, a year, then two years, and many more have gone by. There are only four seasons to keep track of and they come and go, leaving years behind them while continuously ushering in new ones.

I had accepted long ago that people's lives would continue during my incarceration, that my niece and nephew would continue to grow and wouldn't be the small kids they were when I left. But to now see them as older people, going through rites of passage as they graduate from their respective schools and embark on adulthood, looking to chart their own paths and pursue their aspirations is a bit surreal for me. I've received plenty of pictures of them through the years and have been fortunate enough to visit with them as well, but the severe void and longing that swept over me as I looked back to ponder how much of their lives I've missed had never been so stark as it was today.

It's been fourteen years and counting since I've left them! I don't know whether to be somewhat excited that this much time has passed without me agonizing over my sentence, or if I should be dismayed at the fact I've missed so many important things in people's lives while I continue to wish my life away until my release. It's one thing to rationally and consciously understand the fact that I'd be spending over seventeen years of my life in prison, but it's an entirely different level of comprehension now that I've physically seen it manifest in the lives and events of the people that I'm close to.

Time sure does fly. Time flies when you're busy, having fun or, yes, even "doing time." Time flies the older we get, the older our kids get, or God forbid, if you become a grandparent long before you'd like! It almost seems like time doesn't even need a reason to fly — it just takes off at rapid speed when it feels good and ready. Perhaps the only way to "slow down" time is to acknowledge and appreciate each day as its own mini blessing or gift. This way you can have an accumulation of days that you can look back on with gratitude and appreciation. And then maybe, just maybe, you won't wake up one day and say to yourself, "Where has the time gone?"

A FISH OUT OF WATER

When I came to prison, camera phones were the latest phenomenon. My Space was the primary social networking website in use, and Internet apps – what was that? My niece was only one year old, my parents were alive and well, and the economy was thriving.

Fast forward now ten years and it seems there is a new and improved iPhone emerging every few months (by the way, I have no idea what differentiates an iPhone from a Smart phone). These phones, so I'm told, come equipped with Internet access, are able to film videos, and have the ability to swipe credit cards for payment — *wow!*

In conjunction with these advancements in technology that the passage of time has brought about, my parents, sadly, have passed on, my niece is now twelve years old, and our economy is still undergoing a slow but steady recovery. So much has changed. The world seems to be moving at such a rapid pace with technology. Those who were small kids when I left are now teens and adults.

For many of us, we will emerge from prison after having served lengthy sentences and feel like a proverbial fish out of water. The world as we knew it is no more. It has changed several times over in the last ten years, and I have no doubt it will change at least a few more times in the next seven years before I am released.

I often ponder how scary and intimidating it will be during the initial transitional phase as I re-acclimate to society. I get anxious thinking about how out of place I'll feel trying to adjust to such a fast-paced world with advancing technology that is already leaps and bounds above my knowledge and understanding of it. I think of how I will be going from a very structured environment to one where there are no restrictions and I'll be responsible for managing my time throughout the day after seventeen years of "the system" doing it for me. Humans are built with an innate ability to adapt to situations relatively easily, but it still doesn't alleviate the apprehension I feel from the uncertainty posed by new circumstances that inevitably await me upon my release.

The important thing for many of us, however, is knowing we have loving, supportive people out there who will help us every step of the way through this challenging process. As difficult as it will be when I visit my parents' gravesites for the first time, I know my sweetheart will be right there with me, comforting me yet again through a tumultuous time. She will introduce me to the newest model phone and help me devise a professional résumé to submit for employment. I have no doubt that many of you who are reading this will be doing the same for your loved ones upon their release as well.

I thought it was fitting to title this blog "A Fish out of Water" because of its striking metaphorical similarity to the unsettled state we will undergo as we transition back into society. If a fish finds itself in the unfortunate predicament of being taken out of its environment with no one there to pick it up and place it back into water, it will obviously die a relatively slow, agonizing death. Similarly, when we get out of prison we will also be reliant on people around us to come to our aid and help us adjust to the new world we will be a part of. Without this support, we obviously won't literally suffocate and die, but it places the individual under an enormous amount of stress than can translate to destructive, self-defeating criminal behavior as they may feel they have no one to turn to for help. Many will leave prison initially feeling like that poor, helpless fish struggling to breathe outside of the environment that it's comfortable in. I'm just very thankful to know I will undoubtedly have a loving group of people around me who will pick me up and put me back into not the same "water," but a new "body of water" that they will help me navigate and grow accustomed to.

BRANDED

I magine walking around with a sign that says "adulterer," "pathological liar," or "tax evader" plastered to your forehead for all to see. Surely this badge of dishonor would cripple your ability to maintain any type of social life outside of the confines of your home. In other words, walking around wearing a label that identified you by the worst thing you've ever done in life — regardless of how long it's been since you've done it — would render you incapable of living a quality life. This would be your brand, your label by which the world would forever know you and judge you. And this is exactly what we in prison will have to live with for the rest of our lives the day we emerge from prison back into society.

Many who have found themselves in the criminal justice system by way of a felony conviction have and will continue to face the harsh reality that awaits us when we leave prison and seek to rebuild our lives. No doubt we will be denied many of life's most basic essentials: housing, employment, federal financial aid for schooling, and food stamps. Yet, we are expected to reintegrate into a society that wants nothing to do with us. Because of our felony brand that will perpetually stigmatize us, we are precluded from voting in some states. Yet, we are expected to pay taxes and send our kids to schools in districts where we have no right to vote on those tax laws and school policies.

This reality is especially troubling when we often hear how America is the land of opportunity and second chances, discriminating against no one; that if you just work hard and play by the rules, you too can get ahead and build a life for yourself and your family. Apparently, I didn't read the fine print at the bottom of this credo that states, "If you have ever been convicted of a felony — don't even bother — we don't want you anymore!" Principles mean nothing if they are only true in the abstract.

I am of the belief that *most* inmates leave prison with every intention to do the right thing by working to create a productive life for themselves and their families. Who would look to violate the law and return to this dreaded place so soon after release, having just experienced the beauty of freedom after years of confinement? It defies all logic to say the very least. Instead, a more plausible explanation of the high recidivism rate we see in our country is because when door after door has been slammed in our faces at every attempt to legitimately gain solid economic footing, many revert to what they know can yield immediate resources. Crime doesn't pay in the sense of waging one's freedom against it, but it *can* pay the bills in the short term. A principle of survival is that we will do what is necessary to meet our basic needs in the face of seemingly no alternative.

Although I am very passionate about this issue and have no qualms with pointing out the utter counter-productiveness and hypocrisy of the societal practice of discriminating against those who have been convicted of a felony, I would be remiss if I didn't acknowledge the many cities and states that have "banned the box." This means in many cities it is illegal for employers to include on the job application the infamous question we who reside in prison shutter to answer: "Have you ever been convicted of a felony?" Indeed, banning this discriminatory tool will inevitably lead to more opportunity in the realm of employment for many of us, but this is but one arm of the system that works to make it nearly impossible for someone branded a felon to reintegrate in society in a meaningful way. Policies are great, but my optimism in the human spirit calls for something much greater: forgiveness.

Everyone reading this blog has done things they are not proud of and had to ask someone's forgiveness for. We are human and therefore fallible, prone to making mistakes. Obviously, some are more costly than others, but all require forgiveness just the same. We are told our debt to society has been paid once our sentence is up, yet we continue to pay; that doesn't make sense. Once you pay off a credit card debt, you don't *continue* to pay on that debt, do you? Until our collective conscience as a society understands that people are much more than the worst thing they've ever done and are inherently deserving of a second chance, we will continue to isolate, marginalize, and discriminate against a branded demographic of people.

SOMETHING I'LL NEVER ADAPT TO

After a while, even the horrid conditions of prison become normal to its occupants. Waking up every day in a concrete cell, being told when you can shower, use the phone, and even use the bathroom eventually fall into place as routine. No big deal — it just is what it is. I suppose as humans, this is an essential feature and component of our survivability. We must adapt to life's most trying and tumultuous circumstances. Of course, this is usually always preceded by the five phases of grief (denial, anger, bargaining, depression, and finally acceptance) that we undergo; but we do inevitably reach that final phase of acceptance at some point. After which, things tend to settle and become normal again. Yet, the most dreaded, sinking feeling that I've experienced now for the third time in my incarceration last Thursday is something that I will never adapt to. It denies one of the most fundamental needs of humanity and leaves a scar that, unlike those made of flesh, don't fade with time.

When I called home last Thursday (April 21st), I was first greeted with, "Happy Birthday" by none other than my twin brother. Yet, his lackluster tone gave me the sense that something was askew, so I inquired if everything was alright. He paused and then painstakingly told me, "Well, no, it's not alright, Bro . . . [our sister] has passed away." It was an apparent suicide. I hadn't felt that crippling wave of numbness sweep over my body since 2008 when a stoic captain at the prison delivered the news of my father's passing. And now here it was again. Shock, confusion, and devastation paralyzed my mind and body in that moment, and all I could physically muster was an agonizing cry into the phone: "Oh my God! No! No! Oh my God." My brother echoed my anguished cries with his own and we "embraced" each other over the phone just as we had in 2006 when we lost Mom, and 2008 when we lost Dad.

In the days since that fateful Thursday afternoon, all I can think about is how isolated I feel from my family. I am unable to be a source of comfort for them, and they for me, because I am locked in a cage many miles away. We cannot hug, cry on each other's shoulders and whisper, "It's going to be okay; we'll get through this too," because I am confined to a six-by-nine concrete cell for the next five years. Our physical embraces will just have to wait. Not being able to grieve in the aftermath of such a devastating loss is something that I will never adapt to. It is by far the most difficult part of this experience.

When the death of a loved one occurs, it is our innate human instinct and desire to surround ourselves with those who most intimately share our pain and turmoil. It is this profound comfort that soothes our wounds, at least enough to allow us to sleep that night and wake up the next day to do it all over again. But I have been deprived of this fundamental need in my time of immense loss. Instead, I get 30 minutes on the phone to convey how hurt I am and listen to my family's grief. I hang up feeling not as though a cathartic exchange has just taken place, but rather an inadequate one – one that leaves a greater void than the one I had when the phone call started. One that leaves me yearning for more.

On one hand, I am extremely crushed and heartbroken that I cannot physically be with my family during this time of extraordinary grief; yet, I surprisingly feel a sense of solace in knowing that I am still human; that I still possess the basic human quality of desiring close intimacy and compassion from those I love the most in this world during a time of mental and emotional pain. It is comforting, in a sense, to know that twelve and a half years in the cold confines of an institution have not stripped me of my fundamental human nature — the ability to feel. Perhaps this is also why being forbidden to grieve with my family during this time is something I will never adapt to. And this unfortunate reality will forever remain the hardest part of prison for me, and I have no doubt for countless others in this situation.

ADOPT AN INMATE

Several months ago, I was asked by my cellie to fill out a survey for an organization that was looking to glean information from prisoners about our experience. Questions ranged from inquiring how often we receive visits to what type of educational (or otherwise) services are available. Initially I told him I would do it but thought maybe he would not ask me again if I simply stalled and allowed time to pass. A week later he again asked me if I had filled it out yet, and I told him I hadn't but that I would. So, the next day I somewhat begrudgingly filled out the survey, but more or less primarily to appease him and get him off my back.

A couple weeks later I received a response from the self-described "She-EO" of Adopt an Inmate, thanking me for my survey and inviting me to write material for their website. Aside from the intrigue of being able to blog for another site, perhaps what impressed me the most was the fact that this person took the time to *personally* write me back. It's virtually unheard of for an organization that caters to inmates to write in that fashion; rather, it is usually a form letter that you will receive with your name inserted at the beginning. Now that she had my attention, I wanted to know more about what they offered.

After communicating with this organization over the next couple of months, I discovered how unique they are in their approach and commitment to providing services to inmates. Unlike most inmate-based service providers, they don't charge any fees for their services! To say this is not the norm would be a gross understatement. Furthermore, they devote immeasurable time and resources to helping inmates get matched up with people/groups in the community who wish to "adopt" them — or help them get through their time in a meaningful way. This could come in the form of writing letters, acknowledging birthdays and other holidays, receiving phone calls, encouraging education or self-help, etc. Adopters are individuals, churches, and others who are compassionate toward inmates. But there's more.

Adopt an Inmate strongly believes in the necessity of encouraging inmates to write our stories, share our feelings, fears, and ambitions. Thus, they provide us with a platform where we are able to express ourselves through writing, poetry, and various forms of artwork that we can submit for publishing on their website. How awesome it is to see so many pieces of people's lives — their tragedies and triumphs intertwined — decorating a public space in that way! I am incredibly grateful to have had my work displayed on their site and to see the impassioned responses it has garnered. My voice is being heard. The world knows I exist.

To truly appreciate what this organization does and all that their work entails, you would have to see the enormous piles of mail they receive on a *daily* basis from inmates across the nation who are looking to have their work posted, and ultimately to be adopted. It is the head of this organization and her volunteers who spend countless hours typing our hand-written (often in need of much editing) pieces, scanning artwork, processing surveys and classifying inmates by their needs for potential adopters, and responding to every inmate's survey or request.

I now reflect on my initial sentiments regarding being asked to fill out a survey for an organization I assumed was just like all the others — soliciting inmates' money to provide a pen pal service or something similar — and think, boy, was I wrong! But more than that, I think of how necessary such organizations are in a country that incarcerates more people than any other on earth. I think of how many lives (both inmates and those outside who adopt us) will be forever changed through the extraordinary work they do.

When parents are looking to adopt children, they are simply looking to pour all the love they have into nurturing that child, providing a life for the child that they otherwise would have been deprived of. In many ways, they change the trajectory of that person's life and in the process instill a sense of worthiness and importance. Well, after getting to know the all-volunteer staff at Adopt an Inmate, I cannot think of a more suitable name for their organization with the remarkable, altruistic work they do for inmates.

LETTER TO MY YOUNGER SELF

Dear Martin,

I write to you from the other side — the side that awaits you if you don't change your course of action soon.

I know you are going through an extremely tough time right now as you seek independence and try to figure out your identity. Most teenagers find themselves doing the same thing. Your friends are very influential right now, and I understand that no one wants to be shunned by their peers, but please believe me when I say what you have been doing to impress them and gain acceptance is NOT who you are and will only lead you down a path of self-destruction.

I know you started drinking because you are very shy and wanted to come out of your shell and be more sociable, especially when it comes to talking to girls, but if you knew what I know, you would stop right now. You wouldn't pick up another drink if you knew you would become a full-blown alcoholic within the next two years. Martin, you're better than that! You're smarter than that and have the potential to do so much more than what you're currently doing. You can make it in this world by pursuing what makes you happy — not what others want or expect you to do.

You have so much potential. I see it beneath your bravado, tough-guy exterior. You don't have to put up this facade with me — I know you . . . better than you think. You're not a gangster, thug, or tough guy — who are you kidding?! I know you're passionate about art and writing, so why not pursue those things with everything in you? Trust me, you will not regret taking this path in life; it sure beats the alternative — the one that surely awaits you if you stay on this destructive path you're currently on.

Man, if you only knew the pain that you're putting your mom through by going to jail for those stolen-car joyrides you and your brother have been going on with your so-called friends. Are you crazy?! You're already putting yourself in a category that makes it more likely you'll end up in prison than in college! How do you think your mom will feel about that? Believe me, Martin, her pain will be immense. In fact, it very well could contribute to her death some years from now. You don't want that on your conscience, to say the very least, do you? But imagine how happy she would be if you did what you've always talked about doing, going to college to become an architect.

You don't want to be where I am, where you'll be told when you can shower, use the phone, watch TV, eat, and go to bed. You don't want to miss your niece's and nephew's birthdays and Christmases for the next seventeen and a half years, do you? It is beyond demoralizing to have to watch them grow up through pictures and visits every six months or so. Trust me, that would make you regret every decision you are currently making in your life, Martin.

There are countless men where I am who routinely reflect on their lives when they were your age, expressing how they wished they had made different choices that would have kept them from this dreaded place. I am amongst them. I pray you change your behavior soon, so you're not counted among us as well. I beg of you to change before it's too late!

I see what you and your friends do. Where do you think that will lead you? Seriously, I want you to take a moment and ponder where you think those things will get you. Do you think there is a future in doing drugs, drinking, and stealing? Look around you; give me the name of one successful alcoholic or drug addict! Listen, I'm not here to lecture you; I never liked that either when I was your age, but as I now sit here in a concrete cell staring out of a narrow window into a courtyard with a basketball hoop and barbed wire,

MY PRISON LIFE

a huge part of me wishes I had paid attention to what those older people were trying to tell me. Clearly, they knew things I didn't, even though I thought I knew all that I needed to know. I only tell you these things because I love you and don't want to see you end up here — this dreaded place that surely awaits you if you keep on your treacherous path. They even already have a number assigned to you if, and when, you show up here.

I want you to reject what those who claim to be your friends want you to do because when you really think about it, you should be able to clearly see they don't have your best interest at heart. Be true to yourself, believe in yourself, and give yourself a chance — you deserve it. Deny these people the opportunity of ever being able to use that state inmate identification number — ever!

Love,

Your Older Incarcerated Self

View Martin's story on YouTube
"DUI Victim Impact Panel Speech by Martin Lockett"

Made in United States
Troutdale, OR
07/05/2024